Instant Pot®
COOKBOOK

Publications International, Ltd.

Pictured on the front cover: Buffalo Chicken Wings *(page 58)*.

Pictured on the back cover: Pesto Turkey Meatballs *(page 76)*.

ISBN: 978-1-64030-828-2

Manufactured in China.

8 7 6 5 4 3 2 1

CONTENTS

INTRODUCTION

WELCOME TO THE WONDERFUL WORLD OF INSTANT POT COOKING!

Although the current craze makes it seem like a new invention, pressure cooking has actually been around for a few hundred years. Many people grew up hearing frightening stories of pressure cooker catastrophes—exploding pots and soup on the ceiling—but those days are long gone. There have been great changes and improvements in recent years to make modern pressure cookers completely safe, quiet and easy to use. And multi-cookers like the Instant Pot can also do a whole range of additional functions that standard pressure cookers simply can't do.

WHAT EXACTLY IS A PRESSURE COOKER?

It's a simple concept: Liquid is heated in a heavy pot with a lid that locks and forms an airtight seal. Since the steam from the hot liquid is trapped inside and can't evaporate, the pressure increases and raises the boiling point of the contents in the pot, and these items cook faster at a higher temperature. In general, pressure cooking can reduce cooking time to about one third of the time used in conventional cooking methods—and typically the time spent on pressure cooking is hands off. (There's no peeking or stirring when food is being cooked under pressure.)

WHAT MAKES THE INSTANT POT DIFFERENT?

The Instant Pot is a versatile electric multi-cooker that can be a pressure cooker, rice cooker, slow cooker, steamer and yogurt maker. The cooking programs you'll find on the control panel are convenient shortcuts for some foods you may prepare regularly (rice, beans, etc.) which use preset times and cooking levels. But in these pages we'll explore the basics of pressure cooking with recipes that primarily use the Pressure Cook or Manual button along with customized cooking times and pressure levels. These simple and delicious dishes will inspire you to use your Instant Pot daily and create your own Instant Pot magic!

INSTANT POT COMPONENTS

The **exterior pot** is where the electrical components are housed. It should never be immersed in water; to clean it, simply unplug the unit, wipe it with a damp cloth and dry it immediately.

The **inner pot** holds the food and fits snugly into the exterior pot. Made of stainless steel, it is removable, and it can be washed by hand or in the dishwasher.

The **LED display** shows a time that indicates where the pressure cooker is in a particular function. The time counts down to zero from the number of minutes that were programmed. (The timing begins once the machine reaches pressure.) For Keep Warm and Yogurt functions, the time counts up.

The **pressure release valve** is on top of the lid and is used to seal the pot or release steam. To seal the pot, move the valve to the Sealing position; to release pressure, move the valve to the Venting position. This valve can pop off to clean, and to make sure nothing is blocking it.

The **float valve** controls the amount of pressure inside the pressure cooker and indicates when pressure cooking is taking place. The valve rises once the contents of the pot reach working pressure; it drops down when all the pressure has been released after cooking.

The **anti-block shield** is a small stainless steel cage found on the inside of the lid that prevents the pressure cooker from clogging. It can be removed for cleaning.

The **silicone sealing ring** underneath the lid helps create a tight seal to facilitate pressure cooking. The sealing ring has a tendency to absorb strong odors from cooking (particularly from acidic ingredients); washing it regularly with warm soapy water or in the dishwasher will help these odors dissipate, as will storing your Instant Pot with the lid ring side up. If you cook both sweet and savory dishes frequently, you may want to purchase an extra sealing ring (so the scent of curry or pot roast doesn't affect your rice pudding or crème brûlée). Make sure to inspect the ring before cooking—if it has any splits or cracks, it will not work properly and should be replaced.

INSTANT POT COOKING BASICS

Every recipe is slightly different, but most include these basic steps. Read through the entire recipe before beginning to cook so you'll know what ingredients to add and when to add them, which pressure level to use, the cooking time and the release method.

1. Sauté: Many recipes call for sautéing vegetables or browning meat at the beginning of a recipe to add flavor. (Be sure to leave the lid off in this step.)

2. Add the ingredients as the recipe directs and secure the lid, making sure the arrow mark on the lid is aligned with the "close" mark and lock icon on the rim of the outside pot. Turn the pressure release valve to the Sealing position.

3. Select Pressure Cook or Manual, then choose the pressure level. The default setting is high pressure, which is what most recipes in this book use. To change to low pressure, use the Adjust or Pressure Level button. To set the cooking time, use the + and - buttons. The Instant Pot will start automatically.

4. Once the pressure cooking is complete, use the pressure release method directed by the recipe.

THERE ARE THREE TYPES OF RELEASES

NATURAL RELEASE Let the pressure slowly release on its own, which can take anywhere from 5 to 25 minutes (but is typically in the 10- to 15-minute range). The release time will be shorter for a pot that is less full and longer for one that is more full. When the float valve lowers, the pressure is released and you can open the lid.

QUICK RELEASE Use a towel or pot holder to manually turn the pressure release valve to the Venting position immediately after the cooking is complete. Be sure to get out of the way of the steam, and position the pressure cooker on your countertop so the steam doesn't get expelled straight into your cabinets (or in your face). It can take up to 2 minutes to fully release all the pressure.

NATURAL & QUICK RELEASE COMBO The recipe will instruct you to let the pressure release naturally for a certain amount of time (frequently for 10 minutes), and then do a quick release as directed.

TIPS, TRICKS, DOS AND DON'TS

- Read the manual before beginning. There may be features you won't use, but it will eliminate some beginner's confusion and it can help you understand how the Instant Pot works—and see all its possibilities. Models also change over time, so the manual can provide the best information about the buttons and functions of your pot. (Note that the terms "Pressure Cook" and "Manual" are interchangeable.)

- Don't overfill the pot—the total amount of food and liquid should not exceed the maximum level marked on the inner pot. Generally it is best not to fill the pot more than two thirds full; when cooking foods that expand during cooking such as beans and grains, do not fill it more than half full.

- Make sure there is always some liquid in the pot before cooking because a minimum amount is required to come up to pressure (the amount varies between models). However, if the recipe contains a large quantity of vegetables or meats, you may be able to use a bit less since these ingredients will create their own liquid.

- Always check that the pressure release valve is in the right position before you start pressure cooking. The food simply won't get cooked if the valve is not in the Sealing position because there will not be enough pressure in the pot.

- Never try to force the lid open after cooking—if the lid won't open, that means the pressure has not fully released. (As a safety feature, the lid remains locked until the float valve drops down.)

- Save the thickeners for after the pressure cooking is done. Pressure cooker recipes often end up with a lot of flavorful liquid left in the pot; flour or cornstarch mixtures can thicken these liquids into delicious sauces. Use the Sauté function while incorporating the thickeners into the cooking liquid, then cook and stir until the desired consistency is reached.

- Keep in mind that cooking times in some recipes may vary. We've included pressure cooking time charts as a guide (pages 244–249), but these are approximate times, and numerous variables may cause your results to be different. For example, the freshness of dried beans affects their cooking time (older beans take longer to cook), as does what they are cooked with—hard water, acidic ingredients, sugar and salt levels can also affect cooking times. So be flexible and experiment with what works best for you—you can always check the doneness of your food and add more time.

- Set reasonable expectations, i.e., don't expect everything you cook in the Instant Pot to be ready in a few minutes. Even though it reduces many conventional cooking times dramatically, nothing is literally "instant"—it will always take time to get up to pressure, and then to release it. (These machines are fast but not magical!)

RIBOLLITA (TUSCAN BREAD SOUP)

2 tablespoons olive oil

1 onion, halved and thinly sliced

2 stalks celery, diced

1 large carrot, julienned

3 cloves garlic, minced

1½ teaspoons salt

1 teaspoon Italian seasoning

1 bay leaf

¼ teaspoon black pepper

¼ teaspoon red pepper flakes (optional)

4 cups vegetable broth

1 can (28 ounces) whole tomatoes, undrained, coarsely chopped

1 can (about 15 ounces) cannellini beans, rinsed and drained

1 bunch kale, stemmed and coarsely chopped *or* 3 cups thinly sliced cabbage

8 ounces rustic Italian bread, cubed (½-inch pieces)

2 medium zucchini, thinly sliced

1 medium yellow squash, thinly sliced

Shredded Parmesan cheese (optional)

1. Press Sauté; heat oil in Instant Pot. Add onion, celery and carrot; cook and stir 5 minutes. Add garlic, salt, Italian seasoning, bay leaf, black pepper and red pepper flakes, if desired; cook and stir 1 minute. Stir in broth, tomatoes with juice and beans; mix well.

2. Secure lid and move pressure release valve to Sealing position. Press Pressure Cook or Manual; cook at high pressure 8 minutes. When cooking is complete, press Cancel and use quick release.

3. Add kale, bread, zucchini and yellow squash to pot. Secure lid and move pressure release valve to sealing position. Cook at high pressure 1 minute.

4. When cooking is complete, press Cancel and use quick release. Remove and discard bay leaf. Serve with cheese, if desired.

Makes 6 to 8 servings

MIDDLE EASTERN LENTIL SOUP

2 tablespoons olive oil

1 small onion, chopped

1 medium red bell pepper, chopped

1 teaspoon whole fennel seeds

½ teaspoon ground cumin

¼ teaspoon ground red pepper

4 cups water

1 cup dried lentils, rinsed and sorted

1½ teaspoons salt

1 tablespoon lemon juice

½ cup plain yogurt

2 tablespoons chopped fresh parsley

1. Press Sauté; heat oil in Instant Pot. Add onion and bell pepper; cook and stir 3 minutes or until vegetables are softened. Add fennel seeds, cumin and ground red pepper; cook and stir 1 minute. Stir in water, lentils and salt; mix well.

2. Secure lid and move pressure release valve to Sealing position. Press Pressure Cook or Manual; cook at high pressure 17 minutes.

3. When cooking is complete, use natural release for 10 minutes, then release remaining pressure.

4. Stir in lemon juice. Top soup with yogurt; sprinkle with parsley.

Makes 4 servings

CHICKEN ORZO SOUP

1 tablespoon vegetable oil

1 onion, chopped

1 bulb fennel, quartered, cored and thinly sliced (reserve fronds for garnish)

2 teaspoons minced garlic

6 cups chicken broth

1½ pounds boneless skinless chicken breasts

2 carrots, peeled and cut into ¼-inch slices

2 sprigs fresh thyme

1 bay leaf

¾ teaspoon salt

¼ teaspoon black pepper

½ cup uncooked orzo

1. Press Sauté; heat oil in Instant Pot. Add onion and fennel; cook and stir about 6 minutes or until tender. Add garlic; cook and stir 1 minute. Add broth, chicken, carrots, thyme, bay leaf, salt and pepper; mix well.

2. Secure lid and move pressure release valve to Sealing position. Press Pressure Cook or Manual; cook at high pressure 9 minutes.

3. When cooking is complete, use natural release for 10 minutes, then release remaining pressure. Remove chicken to plate; let stand until cool enough to handle.

4. Meanwhile, press Sauté; add orzo to pot. Cook about 10 minutes or until orzo is tender. Remove and discard thyme sprigs and bay leaf.

5. Shred chicken into bite-size pieces. Return chicken to pot; mix well. Garnish soup with fennel fronds.

Makes 6 to 8 servings

FRENCH ONION SOUP

¼ cup (½ stick) butter

4 medium yellow onions (about 3 pounds), sliced

1 tablespoon sugar

¾ teaspoon salt

¼ teaspoon black pepper

¼ cup dry white wine or sherry

8 cups beef broth

8 to 16 slices French bread

1 cup (4 ounces) shredded Gruyere or Swiss cheese

1. Press Sauté; melt butter in Instant Pot. Add onions; cook 15 minutes, stirring occasionally. Add sugar, salt and pepper; cook and stir 5 to 7 minutes or until onions are golden brown. Add wine; cook and stir 1 minute or until evaporated. Stir in broth; mix well.

2. Secure lid and move pressure release valve to Sealing position. Press Pressure Cook or Manual; cook at high pressure 5 minutes.

3. When cooking is complete, press Cancel and use quick release. Preheat broiler.

4. Ladle soup into individual ovenproof bowls; top with 1 or 2 slices bread and about 2 tablespoons cheese. Place bowls on large baking sheet. Broil 1 to 2 minutes or until bread is toasted and cheese is melted and browned.

Makes 8 servings

TURKEY VEGETABLE RICE SOUP

6   cups cold water

2   pounds turkey drumsticks (3 small)

1   large onion, cut into 8 wedges

4   tablespoons soy sauce, divided

1   bay leaf

½   teaspoon salt, divided

½   teaspoon black pepper, divided

2   carrots, sliced

8   ounces mushrooms, sliced

2   cups coarsely chopped bok choy
     (about 6 ounces)

½   cup uncooked rice

1½   cups fresh snow peas, cut in half
     crosswise

1. Combine water, turkey, onion, 2 tablespoons soy sauce, bay leaf, ¼ teaspoon salt and ¼ teaspoon pepper in Instant Pot.

2. Secure lid and move pressure release valve to Sealing position. Press Pressure Cook or Manual; cook at high pressure 25 minutes.

3. When cooking is complete, use natural release for 10 minutes, then release remaining pressure. Remove turkey to plate; let stand until cool enough to handle.

4. Meanwhile, add carrots, mushrooms, bok choy, rice and remaining ¼ teaspoon salt to soup; mix well. Secure lid and move pressure release valve to Sealing position. Press Pressure Cook or Manual; cook at high pressure 4 minutes. When cooking is complete, use natural release for 5 minutes, then release remaining pressure. Remove and discard bay leaf.

5. Remove turkey meat from bones; discard skin and bones. Cut turkey into bite-size pieces. Press Sauté; stir turkey, snow peas, remaining 2 tablespoons soy sauce and ¼ teaspoon pepper into soup. Cook and stir 2 to 3 minutes or until snow peas are crisp-tender.

Makes 6 to 8 servings

CURRIED PARSNIP SOUP

2 tablespoons butter or olive oil

1 medium yellow onion, chopped

2 stalks celery, diced

3 cloves garlic, minced

1 tablespoon salt

2 teaspoons curry powder

½ teaspoon grated fresh ginger

½ teaspoon black pepper

3 pounds parsnips, peeled and cut into 2-inch pieces

6 cups vegetable or chicken broth

Chopped fresh chives (optional)

1. Press Sauté; melt butter in Instant Pot. Add onion and celery; cook and stir 5 minutes or until onion is translucent. Add garlic, salt, curry powder, ginger and pepper; cook and stir 1 minute. Stir in parsnips and broth; mix well.

2. Secure lid and move pressure release valve to Sealing position. Press Pressure Cook or Manual; cook at high pressure 10 minutes.

3. When cooking is complete, use natural release for 10 minutes, then release remaining pressure.

4. Use immersion blender to blend soup until smooth. (Or purée soup in batches in food processor or blender.) Garnish with chives.

Makes 6 to 8 servings

SPICY SQUASH AND CHICKEN SOUP

1 tablespoon vegetable oil

1 small onion, finely chopped

1 stalk celery, finely chopped

2 cups chicken broth

2 cups cubed butternut squash
   (1-inch pieces)

1 can (about 14 ounces) diced tomatoes
   with chiles

8 ounces boneless skinless chicken thighs,
   cut into ½-inch pieces

½ teaspoon salt

½ teaspoon ground ginger

⅛ teaspoon ground cumin

⅛ teaspoon black pepper

2 teaspoons lime juice

½ to 1 teaspoon hot pepper sauce

   Fresh cilantro or parsley sprigs (optional)

1. Press Sauté; heat oil in Instant Pot. Add onion and celery; cook and stir 4 minutes or until vegetables are softened. Add broth, squash, tomatoes, chicken, salt, ginger, cumin and black pepper; mix well.

2. Secure lid and move pressure release valve to Sealing position. Press Pressure Cook or Manual; cook at high pressure 5 minutes.

3. When cooking is complete, use natural release for 10 minutes, then release remaining pressure.

4. Stir in lime juice and hot pepper sauce; garnish with cilantro.

Makes 4 servings

TOMATO BASIL SOUP

1 tablespoon olive oil

1 medium onion, finely chopped

3 tablespoons tomato paste

1 tablespoon packed dark brown sugar

1 teaspoon salt

¼ teaspoon black pepper

¼ teaspoon ground allspice

1 can (28 ounces) whole tomatoes, undrained, chopped

2 cans (about 14 ounces each) fire-roasted diced tomatoes

2 cups vegetable broth

1 can (5 ounces) evaporated milk

¼ cup chopped fresh basil

1. Press Sauté; heat oil in Instant Pot. Add onion; cook and stir 10 minutes or until dark brown. Add tomato paste, brown sugar, salt, pepper and allspice; cook and stir 1 minute. Stir in whole tomatoes with juice, diced tomatoes and broth; mix well.

2. Secure lid and move pressure release valve to Sealing position. Press Pressure Cook or Manual; cook at high pressure 5 minutes.

3. When cooking is complete, use natural release for 20 minutes, then release remaining pressure.

4. Press Sauté; add evaporated milk and basil to pot. Cook and stir just until heated through.

Makes 6 servings

BEAN AND PASTA SOUP

1¼ cups dried navy beans, soaked 8 hours
   or overnight

3 slices bacon, finely chopped

1 onion, chopped

1 stalk celery, chopped

1 carrot, chopped

2 cloves garlic, minced

4 cups water

1 smoked ham hock (8 to 12 ounces)

½ teaspoon salt

½ teaspoon dried thyme

½ teaspoon dried marjoram

¼ teaspoon black pepper

¾ cup uncooked small pasta shells

2 tablespoons chopped fresh parsley

½ to 1 cup chicken broth (optional)

Grated Parmesan cheese (optional)

1. Drain and rinse beans. Press Sauté; cook bacon in Instant Pot until crisp. Add onion, celery and carrot; cook and stir 5 minutes or until golden brown, scraping up browned bits from bottom of pot. Add garlic; cook and stir 30 seconds. Add beans, water, ham hock, salt, thyme, marjoram and pepper; mix well.

2. Secure lid and move pressure release valve to Sealing position. Press Pressure Cook or Manual; cook at high pressure 16 minutes.

3. When cooking is complete, use natural release for 10 minutes, then release remaining pressure.

4. Remove ham hock to plate. Use immersion blender to partially purée soup, leaving soup chunky. (Or remove half of soup to food processor or blender; process until smooth and return puréed soup to pot.)

5. Press Sauté; bring soup to a boil. Stir in pasta. Adjust heat to low ("less"); cook about 10 minutes or until pasta is tender, stirring occasionally.

6. Meanwhile, remove meat from ham hock; chop into bite-size pieces. Stir meat and parsley into soup. If necessary, thin soup with broth. Serve with cheese, if desired.

Makes 4 servings

POZOLE

1 tablespoon olive oil

1 large onion, halved then cut into ¼-inch slices

2 teaspoons dried oregano

1 clove garlic, minced

½ teaspoon ground cumin

12 ounces boneless skinless chicken thighs, cut into 1-inch strips

2 cans (4 ounces each) chopped green chiles

3 cups chicken broth

¼ teaspoon salt

1 package (10 ounces) frozen corn

1 can (2¼ ounces) sliced black olives, drained

Chopped fresh cilantro (optional)

Lime wedges (optional)

1. Press Sauté; heat oil in Instant Pot. Add onion; cook and stir about 5 minutes or until softened. Add oregano, garlic and cumin; cook and stir 1 minute. Stir in chicken and chiles until blended. Add broth and salt; mix well.

2. Secure lid and move pressure release valve to Sealing position. Press Pressure Cook or Manual; cook at high pressure 5 minutes.

3. When cooking is complete, use natural release for 10 minutes, then release remaining pressure.

4. Press Sauté; add corn and olives to soup. Cook and stir 3 minutes or until heated through. Garnish with cilantro; serve with lime wedges, if desired.

Makes 6 servings

CREAMY CARROT SOUP

1 tablespoon butter
½ cup chopped onion
1 tablespoon chopped fresh ginger
1 pound baby carrots or regular carrots, cut into 2-inch pieces
½ teaspoon salt
¼ teaspoon black pepper

3 cups vegetable broth
¼ cup whipping cream
2 tablespoons orange juice
Pinch ground nutmeg
4 tablespoons sour cream (optional)
Fresh parsley sprigs (optional)

1. Press Sauté; melt butter in Instant Pot. Add onion and ginger; cook and stir 1 minute or until ginger is fragrant. Add carrots, salt and pepper; cook and stir 2 minutes. Stir in broth; mix well.

2. Secure lid and move pressure release valve to Sealing position. Press Pressure Cook or Manual; cook at high pressure 6 minutes.

3. When cooking is complete, use natural release for 10 minutes, then release remaining pressure.

4. Use immersion blender to blend soup until smooth. (Or purée soup in batches in food processor or blender.)

5. Press Sauté; adjust heat to low ("less"). Add cream, orange juice and nutmeg; cook until heated through, stirring frequently. (Do not boil.) Top with sour cream and parsley, if desired.

Makes 4 servings

NORTH AFRICAN CHICKEN SOUP

1 tablespoon vegetable oil

1 cup chopped onion

3 cloves garlic, minced

¾ teaspoon paprika

½ teaspoon ground cumin

½ teaspoon ground ginger

¼ teaspoon ground allspice

1¼ pounds peeled sweet potatoes, cut into 1-inch pieces (2½ cups)

2 cups chicken broth

1 can (about 14 ounces) whole tomatoes, undrained, cut up or crushed with hands

12 ounces boneless skinless chicken thighs, cut into 1-inch pieces

½ teaspoon salt

¼ to ½ teaspoon black pepper

Hot pepper sauce and lime juice (optional)

1. Press Sauté; heat oil in Instant Pot. Add onion; cook and stir 3 minutes or until softened. Add garlic; cook and stir 30 seconds. Add paprika, cumin, ginger and allspice; cook and stir 30 seconds. Add sweet potatoes, broth, tomatoes with juice, chicken and salt; mix well.

2. Secure lid and move pressure release valve to Sealing position. Press Pressure Cook or Manual; cook at high pressure 5 minutes.

3. When cooking is complete, use natural release for 10 minutes, then release remaining pressure. Stir in black pepper to taste. Serve with hot pepper sauce and lime juice, if desired.

Makes 4 to 6 servings (6 cups)

MINESTRONE ALLA MILANESE

¾ **cup dried cannellini beans, soaked 8 hours or overnight**

2 **tablespoons olive oil**

1 **cup chopped carrots (½-inch pieces)**

1 **stalk celery, halved lengthwise and cut crosswise into ¼-inch slices**

¾ **cup chopped onion**

2 **cloves garlic, minced**

1 **container (32 ounces) vegetable broth**

1 **can (about 14 ounces) diced tomatoes**

1 **cup diced unpeeled red potato (about 1 large)**

1 **cup coarsely chopped green cabbage**

1 **small zucchini, halved lengthwise and cut crosswise into ¼-inch slices**

¾ **cup sliced fresh green beans**

1½ **teaspoons salt**

½ **teaspoon dried basil**

¼ **teaspoon dried rosemary**

¼ **teaspoon black pepper**

1 **bay leaf**

Shredded Parmesan cheese (optional)

1. Drain and rinse dried beans. Press Sauté; heat oil in Instant Pot. Add carrots, celery and onion; cook and stir 5 minutes or until vegetables are softened. Add garlic; cook and stir 1 minute. Stir in broth, tomatoes, potato, cabbage, zucchini, green beans, salt, basil, rosemary, pepper and bay leaf; mix well.

2. Secure lid and move pressure release valve to Sealing position. Press Pressure Cook or Manual; cook at high pressure 10 minutes.

3. When cooking is complete, use natural release for 15 minutes, then release remaining pressure. Remove and discard bay leaf. Garnish with cheese.

Makes 6 servings

SPLIT PEA SOUP

8 slices bacon, chopped

1 onion, chopped

2 carrots, chopped

1 stalk celery, chopped

1 clove garlic, minced

½ teaspoon dried thyme

1 container (32 ounces) chicken broth

2 cups water

1 package (16 ounces) dried split peas, rinsed and sorted

¾ teaspoon salt

½ teaspoon black pepper

1 bay leaf

1. Press Sauté; cook and stir bacon in Instant Pot until crisp. Remove to paper towel-lined plate. Drain off all but 1 tablespoon drippings.

2. Add onion, carrots and celery to pot; cook and stir 5 minutes or until vegetables are softened. Add garlic and thyme; cook and stir 1 minute. Stir in broth and water, scraping up browned bits from bottom of pot. Add split peas, half of bacon, salt, pepper and bay leaf; mix well.

3. Secure lid and move pressure release valve to Sealing position. Press Pressure Cook or Manual; cook at high pressure 8 minutes.

4. When cooking is complete, use natural release for 10 minutes, then release remaining pressure. Stir soup; remove and discard bay leaf. Garnish with remaining bacon.

Makes 4 to 6 servings

NOTE: The soup may seem thin immediately after cooking, but it will thicken upon standing. If prepared in advance and refrigerated, thin the soup with water when reheating until it reaches the desired consistency.

OXTAIL SOUP

2½ pounds meaty beef oxtails

1 large onion, halved and sliced

4 carrots, cut into ¾-inch pieces, divided

3 stalks celery, cut into ¾-inch pieces, divided

2 sprigs fresh parsley

2 cloves garlic, peeled

½ teaspoon salt

1 bay leaf

5 whole black peppercorns

2 cups beef broth

1 cup dark beer or stout

1 large russet potato, cut into 1-inch pieces

Ground black pepper

Chopped fresh parsley (optional)

1. Combine oxtails, onion, half of carrots, one third of celery, parsley sprigs, garlic, ½ teaspoon salt, bay leaf and peppercorns in Instant Pot. Stir in broth and beer.

2. Secure lid and move pressure release valve to Sealing position. Press Pressure Cook or Manual; cook at high pressure 35 minutes.

3. When cooking is complete, use natural release for 5 minutes, then release remaining pressure. Remove oxtails to plate.

4. Strain broth through large sieve or colander, pressing vegetables with slotted spoon to extract all liquid. Discard vegetables. Wipe out pot with paper towels, if necessary. Return broth to pot with remaining half of carrots, two thirds of celery and potato.

5. Secure lid and move pressure release valve to Sealing position. Press Pressure Cook or Manual; cook at high pressure 3 minutes. When cooking is complete, press Cancel and use quick release.

6. Remove meat from oxtails when cool enough to handle, discarding fat and bones. Press Sauté; add meat to soup. Cook 2 minutes or until heated through. Season with additional salt and pepper; garnish with chopped parsley.

Makes 4 servings

VEGETABLE BEAN SOUP

1 cup dried Great Northern beans, soaked 8 hours or overnight

1 tablespoon olive oil

1 cup chopped onion

¾ cup chopped carrots

3 cloves garlic, minced

4 cups coarsely chopped green cabbage

4 cups coarsely chopped unpeeled red potatoes (about 4 medium)

1 teaspoon dried rosemary

4 cups vegetable broth

1 can (about 14 ounces) diced tomatoes

1½ teaspoons salt

½ teaspoon black pepper

Grated Parmesan cheese (optional)

1. Rinse and drain beans. Press Sauté; heat oil in Instant Pot. Add onion and carrots; cook and stir 3 minutes or until vegetables are softened. Add garlic; cook and stir 30 seconds. Add cabbage, potatoes and rosemary; cook and stir 1 minute. Stir in beans, broth, tomatoes, salt and pepper; mix well.

2. Secure lid and move pressure release valve to Sealing position. Press Pressure Cook or Manual; cook at high pressure 7 minutes.

3. When cooking is complete, use natural release for 10 minutes, then release remaining pressure. Serve with cheese, if desired.

Makes 6 to 8 servings

CHICKEN TORTILLA SOUP

2   cans (about 14 ounces each) diced tomatoes

1½ pounds boneless skinless chicken thighs

1   onion, chopped

½   cup chicken broth

1   can (4 ounces) diced green chiles

2   cloves garlic, minced

1   teaspoon salt

1   teaspoon ground cumin

¼   teaspoon black pepper

4   corn tortillas, cut into ¼-inch strips

2   tablespoons chopped fresh cilantro

½   cup (2 ounces) shredded Monterey Jack cheese

1   avocado, diced and tossed with lime juice

    Lime wedges

1. Combine tomatoes, chicken, onion, broth, chiles, garlic, salt, cumin and pepper in Instant Pot; mix well.

2. Secure lid and move pressure release valve to Sealing position. Press Pressure Cook or Manual; cook at high pressure 9 minutes.

3. When cooking is complete, use natural release for 10 minutes, then release remaining pressure.

4. Remove chicken to plate; shred into bite-size pieces when cool enough to handle. Stir into soup.

5. Press Sauté; add tortillas and cilantro to soup. Cook and stir 2 minutes or until heated through. Top with cheese, avocado and squeeze of lime juice. Serve immediately.*

If desired, soup can be made ahead through step 3. When ready to serve, heat soup to a simmer; add tortilla strips and cilantro and cook until heated through.

Makes 4 to 6 servings

HERB LEMON TURKEY BREAST

½ **cup lemon juice**

½ **cup dry white wine**

4 **cloves garlic, minced**

1 **teaspoon salt**

½ **teaspoon dried parsley flakes**

½ **teaspoon dried tarragon**

½ **teaspoon dried rosemary**

¼ **teaspoon ground sage**

¼ **teaspoon black pepper**

1 **boneless turkey breast (about 3 pounds)**

Fresh herbs and lemon slices (optional)

1. Combine lemon juice, wine, garlic, salt, parsley flakes, tarragon, dried rosemary, sage and pepper in measuring cup or small bowl; mix well.

2. Place turkey breast in Instant Pot; pour juice mixture over turkey, turning to coat. (Turkey should be right side up for cooking.)

3. Secure lid and move pressure release valve to Sealing position. Press Pressure Cook or Manual; cook at high pressure 30 minutes.

4. When cooking is complete, use natural release for 10 minutes, then release remaining pressure. Remove turkey to cutting board; tent with foil. Let stand 10 minutes before slicing.

5. Use cooking liquid as sauce, if desired, or thicken liquid with flour (see Tip). Garnish as desired.

Makes 4 servings

TIP: If desired, prepare gravy with cooking liquid after removing turkey from pot. Place ¼ cup all-purpose flour in small bowl; stir in ½ cup cooking liquid until smooth. Press Sauté; add flour mixture to pot. Cook 5 minutes or until gravy thickens, stirring frequently.

CHICKEN CACCIATORE

¼ cup all-purpose flour

½ teaspoon salt

¼ teaspoon black pepper

3 pounds boneless skinless chicken breasts

1 tablespoon olive oil

1 cup onion, sliced

½ cup water

2 teaspoons garlic powder

1 teaspoon dried oregano

1 teaspoon paprika

1 teaspoon ground cumin

⅛ teaspoon ground red pepper

½ medium red bell pepper, sliced

½ medium green bell pepper, sliced

½ medium yellow bell pepper, sliced

1¼ cups grape tomatoes (about 15)

Hot cooked noodles or rice (optional)

1. Combine flour, salt and black pepper in shallow bowl; mix well. Coat chicken with flour mixture; shake off excess.

2. Press Sauté; heat oil in Instant Pot. Add chicken; cook about 4 minutes per side or until browned. Remove to plate. Add onion; cook and stir 3 minutes or until softened. Add water, garlic powder, oregano, paprika, cumin and ground red pepper; cook and stir 1 minute. Add bell peppers and tomatoes; mix well.

3. Secure lid and move pressure release valve to Sealing position. Press Pressure Cook or Manual; cook at high pressure 10 minutes.

4. When cooking is complete, press Cancel and use quick release.

5. Press Sauté; cook 2 minutes or until sauce thickens slightly. Serve with noodles, if desired.

Makes 6 servings

BRAISED CHICKEN WITH VEGETABLES

¾   cup chicken broth

2   tablespoons lemon juice

2   cloves garlic, minced

1½   teaspoons Italian seasoning

¾   teaspoon cornstarch

½   teaspoon salt

½   teaspoon dried rosemary

½   teaspoon paprika

¼   teaspoon black pepper

4   chicken drumsticks, skin removed

1   yellow squash, cut into ½-inch pieces

1   zucchini, cut into ½-inch pieces

1   onion, cut into ½-inch pieces

1   small red bell pepper, cut into ½-inch pieces

1. Combine broth, lemon juice, garlic, Italian seasoning, cornstarch, salt, rosemary, paprika and black pepper in Instant Pot; mix well. Add chicken; stir to coat.

2. Secure lid and move pressure release valve to Sealing position. Press Pressure Cook or Manual; cook at high pressure 10 minutes.

3. When cooking is complete, press Cancel and use quick release.

4. Add squash, zucchini, onion and bell pepper to pot; press into cooking liquid. Secure lid and move pressure release valve to Sealing position. Press Pressure Cook or Manual; cook at high pressure 1 minute. When cooking is complete, press Cancel and use quick release. Remove chicken and vegetables to platter with slotted spoon; tent with foil.

5. Press Sauté; cook about 5 minutes or until sauce is slightly reduced. Serve sauce over chicken and vegetables.

Makes 2 to 4 servings

HEARTY CHICKEN CHILI

1 tablespoon vegetable oil

1 onion, finely chopped

1 jalapeño pepper, minced

1 clove garlic, minced

1½ teaspoons chili powder

¾ teaspoon salt

½ teaspoon ground cumin

½ teaspoon dried oregano

½ teaspoon black pepper

¼ teaspoon red pepper flakes (optional)

1 cup chicken broth

1½ pounds boneless skinless chicken thighs, cut into 1-inch pieces

2 cans (about 15 ounces each) hominy, rinsed and drained

1 can (about 15 ounces) pinto beans, rinsed and drained

1 tablespoon all-purpose flour (optional)

Chopped fresh cilantro (optional)

1. Press Sauté; heat oil in Instant Pot. Add onion; cook and stir 3 minutes or until softened. Add jalapeño, garlic, chili powder, salt, cumin, oregano, black pepper and red pepper flakes, if desired; cook and stir 30 seconds. Stir in broth; cook 1 minute. Add chicken, hominy and beans; mix well.

2. Secure lid and move pressure release valve to Sealing position. Press Pressure Cook or Manual; cook at high pressure 6 minutes.

3. When cooking is complete, use natural release for 10 minutes, then release remaining pressure.

4. For thicker chili, stir 1 tablespoon flour into 3 tablespoons cooking liquid in small bowl until smooth. Press Sauté; add flour mixture to chili. Cook about 5 minutes or until chili thickens, stirring occasionally. Garnish with cilantro.

Makes 4 servings

CHICKEN CONGEE

4 cups water

4 cups chicken broth

2 chicken leg quarters *or* 4 chicken drumsticks, skin removed (1 to 1½ pounds)

1 cup uncooked white jasmine rice, rinsed well and drained

1 (1-inch) piece fresh ginger, cut into ¼-inch slices

1 teaspoon salt

½ teaspoon white pepper

Optional toppings: soy sauce, sesame oil, sliced green onions, shredded carrot, salted roasted peanuts and/or pickled vegetables

1. Combine water, broth, chicken, rice, ginger, salt and pepper in Instant Pot; mix well.

2. Secure lid and move pressure release valve to Sealing position. Press Pressure Cook or Manual; cook at high pressure 20 minutes.

3. When cooking is complete, use natural release for 15 minutes, then release remaining pressure. Remove and discard ginger. Remove chicken to plate; set aside until cool enough to handle.

4. Meanwhile, press Sauté; cook and stir congee 2 to 3 minutes or until desired consistency is reached. Shred chicken; stir into congee. Serve with desired toppings.

Makes 6 servings

TURKEY ROPA VIEJA

1 tablespoon olive oil

1 onion, thinly sliced

1 green bell pepper, chopped

1 clove garlic, minced

¾ teaspoon ground cumin

½ teaspoon dried oregano

2 medium tomatoes, chopped

1 can (8 ounces) tomato sauce

⅓ cup sliced pimiento-stuffed green olives

½ teaspoon salt

¼ teaspoon black pepper

1 pound turkey tenderloins (2 large or 3 small) *or* 1½ pounds boneless turkey breast, cut into 3 to 4 pieces

1 tablespoon lemon juice

Hot cooked rice and beans (optional)

1. Press Sauté; heat oil in Instant Pot. Add onion and bell pepper; cook and stir 3 minutes or until softened. Add garlic, cumin and oregano; cook and stir 30 seconds. Stir in tomatoes, tomato sauce, olives, salt and black pepper; mix well. Add turkey to pot, pressing into tomato mixture.

2. Secure lid and move pressure release valve to Sealing position. Press Pressure Cook or Manual; cook at high pressure 20 minutes.

3. When cooking is complete, use natural release for 10 minutes, then release remaining pressure. Remove turkey to plate.

4. Press Sauté; cook 10 to 15 minutes or until sauce is reduced by one third.

5. Meanwhile, shred turkey into bite-sized pieces when cool enough to handle. Add turkey and lemon juice to sauce; mix well. Serve with rice and beans, if desired.

Makes 4 servings

BUFFALO CHICKEN WINGS

3 pounds chicken wings, tips discarded, separated at joints

1 teaspoon salt, divided

1 teaspoon garlic powder

½ cup water

⅓ cup butter

⅔ cup hot pepper sauce

1½ teaspoons Worcestershire sauce

1 teaspoon packed brown sugar

Ranch dressing (optional)

Celery sticks (optional)

1. Season wings with ¾ teaspoon salt and garlic powder. Pour water into Instant Pot. Place rack in pot; place wings on rack (or use steamer basket to hold wings).

2. Secure lid and move pressure release valve to Sealing position. Press Pressure Cook or Manual; cook at high pressure 5 minutes.

3. Meanwhile, preheat broiler. Line baking sheet with foil. Microwave butter in large microwavable bowl until melted. Stir in hot pepper sauce, Worcestershire sauce, brown sugar and remaining ¼ teaspoon salt until well blended.

4. When cooking is complete, press Cancel and use quick release. Pat wings dry with paper towels; add to bowl of sauce and toss well to coat. Spread wings in single layer on prepared baking sheet. (Reserve sauce left in bowl.)

5. Broil about 6 minutes or until browned. Turn and brush with remaining sauce; broil 4 to 5 minutes or until browned. Return to bowl with sauce; toss to coat. Serve with ranch dressing and celery, if desired.

Makes 4 to 6 servings

BUTTER CHICKEN

2 tablespoons butter

1 onion, chopped

4 cloves garlic, minced

1 teaspoon minced fresh ginger

1 teaspoon ground turmeric

1 teaspoon ground coriander

1 teaspoon garam masala

1 teaspoon ground cumin

½ teaspoon ground red pepper

½ teaspoon paprika

1 can (about 14 ounces) diced tomatoes

¾ teaspoon salt

2 pounds boneless skinless chicken breasts, cut into 2-inch pieces

½ cup whipping cream

Chopped fresh cilantro

Hot cooked rice (optional)

1. Press Sauté; melt butter in Instant Pot. Add onion; cook and stir about 3 minutes or until onion begins to turn golden. Add garlic and ginger; cook and stir 1 minute. Add turmeric, coriander, garam masala, cumin, red pepper and paprika; cook and stir 30 seconds. Add tomatoes and salt; cook and stir 2 minutes. Stir in chicken; mix well.

2. Secure lid and move pressure release valve to Sealing position. Press Pressure Cook or Manual; cook at high pressure 8 minutes.

3. When cooking is complete, use natural release for 10 minutes, then release remaining pressure.

4. Press Sauté; adjust heat to low ("less"). Stir in cream; cook 5 minutes or until heated through. Sprinkle with cilantro; serve with rice, if desired.

Makes 4 to 6 servings

QUICK CHICKEN AND BEAN STEW

1 **pound boneless skinless chicken thighs, cut into 1-inch pieces**

1 **can (about 15 ounces) Great Northern beans, rinsed and drained**

1 **can (about 15 ounces) black beans, rinsed and drained**

1 **can (about 14 ounces) crushed tomatoes (preferably fire-roasted)**

1 **onion, chopped**

⅓ **cup chicken broth**

Juice of 1 large orange (about ⅓ cup)

1 **canned chipotle pepper in adobo sauce, minced**

1 **teaspoon salt**

1 **teaspoon ground cumin**

1 **bay leaf**

Fresh cilantro sprigs (optional)

1. Combine chicken, beans, tomatoes, onion, broth, orange juice, chipotle pepper, salt, cumin and bay leaf in Instant Pot; mix well.

2. Secure lid and move pressure release valve to Sealing position. Press Pressure Cook or Manual; cook at high pressure 6 minutes.

3. When cooking is complete, use natural release for 5 minutes, then release remaining pressure.

4. Press Sauté; cook 3 to 5 minutes or until stew thickens, stirring frequently. Remove and discard bay leaf. Garnish with cilantro.

Makes 4 to 6 servings

PROVENÇAL LEMON AND OLIVE CHICKEN

2 cups chopped onions

2½ pounds bone-in skinless chicken thighs (about 6)

1 lemon, thinly sliced and seeded

1 cup pitted green olives

1 tablespoon olive brine or white vinegar

2 teaspoons herbes de Provence*

1 bay leaf

1 teaspoon salt

¼ teaspoon black pepper

⅓ cup chicken broth

½ cup minced fresh Italian parsley

Hot cooked rice (optional)

*Or substitute ½ teaspoon each *dried rosemary, thyme, sage and savory.*

1. Place onions in Instant Pot. Arrange chicken over onions; top with lemon slices. Add olives, brine, herbes de Provence, bay leaf, salt and pepper. Pour in broth.

2. Secure lid and move pressure release valve to Sealing position. Press Pressure Cook or Manual; cook at high pressure 10 minutes.

3. When cooking is complete, press Cancel and use quick release. Remove chicken to plate; tent with foil.

4. Press Sauté; cook about 5 minutes or until sauce is reduced by one third. Remove and discard bay leaf; stir in parsley. Serve sauce with chicken and rice, if desired.

Makes 4 servings

COQ AU VIN

4 slices thick-cut bacon, cut into ½-inch pieces

8 bone-in skinless chicken thighs (3½ to 4 pounds)

1 teaspoon salt

½ teaspoon black pepper

1 package (8 to 10 ounces) cremini or white mushrooms, quartered

3 medium carrots, cut into 1½-inch pieces

1 tablespoon tomato paste

2 cloves garlic, minced

10 sprigs fresh thyme

1½ cups dry red wine

8 ounces frozen pearl onions (about 1½ cups), divided

1 bay leaf

1 tablespoon butter, softened

1 tablespoon all-purpose flour

Chopped fresh parsley (optional)

1. Press Sauté; cook bacon in Instant Pot until crisp. Remove to paper towel-lined plate.

2. Season both sides of chicken with 1 teaspoon salt and ½ teaspoon pepper. Add chicken to drippings in pot in two batches; cook 3 to 4 minutes per side or until browned. Remove to plate.

3. Add mushrooms and carrots to pot; cook about 6 minutes or until mushrooms have released their liquid and begin to brown, stirring occasionally and scraping up browned bits from bottom of pot. Add tomato paste, garlic and thyme; cook and stir 2 minutes. Stir in wine; cook about 10 minutes or until reduced by half. Return chicken to pot with half of onions, half of bacon and bay leaf.

4. Secure lid and move pressure release valve to Sealing position. Press Pressure Cook or Manual; cook at high pressure 14 minutes. Meanwhile, mix butter and flour in small bowl until well blended.

5. When cooking is complete, press Cancel and use quick release. Remove chicken and vegetables to platter with slotted spoon. Remove and discard thyme sprigs and bay leaf. Press Sauté; add remaining half of onions and butter mixture to pot. Cook and stir 2 to 3 minutes or until sauce thickens. Season with additional salt and pepper, if desired. Pour sauce over chicken and vegetables. Garnish with reserved bacon and parsley, if desired.

Makes 4 to 6 servings

PULLED TURKEY SANDWICHES

1 tablespoon vegetable oil

1 small red onion, finely chopped

1 can (8 ounces) tomato sauce

¼ cup ketchup

2 tablespoons packed brown sugar

1 tablespoon cider vinegar

2 teaspoons Worcestershire sauce

1 teaspoon Dijon mustard

¼ teaspoon salt

¼ teaspoon chipotle chili powder

1½ pounds turkey tenderloins (2 small), each cut in half

4 sandwich rolls or buns

1. Press Sauté; heat oil in Instant Pot. Add onion; cook and stir 3 minutes or until softened. Add tomato sauce, ketchup, brown sugar, vinegar, Worcestershire sauce, mustard, salt and chili powder; mix well. Cook about 5 minutes or until sauce is reduced and thickened, stirring frequently.

2. Add turkey; turn to coat all sides with sauce. Secure lid and move pressure release valve to Sealing position. Press Pressure Cook or Manual; cook at high pressure 20 minutes.

3. When cooking is complete, use natural release for 10 minutes, then release remaining pressure. Remove turkey to plate; set aside until cool enough to handle.

4. Press Sauté; adjust heat to low ("less"). Cook sauce 8 to 10 minutes or until slightly thickened and reduced. Shred turkey into bite-size pieces; add to sauce and stir until well blended. Serve on rolls.

Makes 4 servings

ITALIAN COUNTRY-STYLE CHICKEN

½ **cup dried porcini mushrooms
   (about ½ ounce)**

1 **cup boiling water**

⅓ **cup all-purpose flour**

1 **teaspoon salt**

½ **teaspoon black pepper**

1 **cut-up whole chicken (3½ to 4 pounds)***

2 **tablespoons olive oil**

1 **medium onion, chopped**

2 **carrots, cut diagonally into ¼-inch slices**

3 **ounces pancetta,** chopped (about
   ½ cup)**

3 **cloves garlic, minced**

1 **tablespoon tomato paste**

1 **cup pitted green Italian olives**

**Or use 2 leg quarters and 2 breasts and cut each
into two pieces.*

**Or substitute 3 ounces bacon.

1. Place mushrooms in small bowl; pour boiling water over mushrooms. Let stand 15 to 20 minutes or until mushrooms are softened. Meanwhile, combine flour, 1 teaspoon salt and ½ teaspoon pepper in large resealable food storage bag. Add 1 or 2 pieces of chicken at a time; toss to coat.

2. Press Sauté; heat oil in Instant Pot. Add chicken in two batches; cook until browned on both sides. Remove to plate. Pour off all but 1 tablespoon fat.

3. Drain mushrooms; reserve and strain soaking liquid. Chop mushrooms. Add onion, carrots and pancetta to pot; cook and stir 5 minutes. Add garlic and tomato paste; cook and stir 1 minute. Add reserved mushroom liquid; cook 2 minutes, scraping up browned bits from bottom of pot. Stir in mushrooms; mix well. Return chicken to pot, pressing into liquid.

4. Secure lid and move pressure release valve to Sealing position. Press Pressure Cook or Manual; cook at high pressure 10 minutes. When cooking is complete, press Cancel and use quick release. Remove chicken to platter; tent with foil.

5. Press Sauté. Add olives; cook about 2 minutes or until heated through and sauce thickens slightly, stirring frequently. Season with additional salt and pepper, if desired. Pour sauce over chicken.

Makes 4 servings

CHINESE CHICKEN STEW

1 **pound boneless skinless chicken thighs, cut into 1-inch pieces**

1 **teaspoon Chinese five-spice powder**

½ **teaspoon red pepper flakes**

¼ **teaspoon salt**

1 **tablespoon peanut or vegetable oil**

1 **onion, coarsely chopped**

1 **package (8 ounces) mushrooms, sliced**

2 **cloves garlic, minced**

⅓ **cup plus 2 tablespoons chicken broth, divided**

1 **tablespoon plus 1 teaspoon soy sauce, divided**

1 **red bell pepper, cut into ½-inch pieces**

2 **green onions, cut into ½-inch pieces**

1 **tablespoon cornstarch**

1 **teaspoon dark sesame oil**

Hot cooked rice

¼ **cup chopped fresh cilantro (optional)**

1. Combine chicken, five-spice powder, red pepper flakes and salt in medium bowl; toss to coat. Press Sauté; heat peanut oil in Instant Pot. Add onion and chicken; cook and stir 5 minutes or until chicken is browned. Add mushrooms and garlic; cook and stir 3 minutes, scraping up browned bits from bottom of pot. Stir in ⅓ cup broth and 1 teaspoon soy sauce; mix well.

2. Secure lid and move pressure release valve to Sealing position. Press Pressure Cook or Manual; cook at high pressure 5 minutes.

3. When cooking is complete, press Cancel and use quick release.

4. Press Sauté; add bell pepper and green onions to pot. Cook 3 minutes, stirring occasionally. Stir remaining 2 tablespoons broth into cornstarch in small bowl until smooth. Add cornstarch mixture to pot with remaining 1 tablespoon soy sauce and sesame oil; cook and stir 2 minutes or until sauce thickens. Serve stew with rice; sprinkle with cilantro, if desired.

Makes 4 servings

CHICKEN ENCHILADA CHILI

1 can (about 14 ounces) diced tomatoes with green chiles

1 can (10 ounces) red enchilada sauce

½ teaspoon salt

¼ teaspoon ground cumin

⅛ teaspoon black pepper

1½ pounds boneless skinless chicken thighs, cut into 1-inch pieces

1 cup frozen or canned corn

1½ tablespoons cornmeal

2 tablespoons finely chopped fresh cilantro

½ cup (2 ounces) shredded pepper jack cheese

Sliced green onions

1. Combine tomatoes, enchilada sauce, salt, cumin and pepper in Instant Pot; mix well. Add chicken; stir to coat.

2. Secure lid and move pressure release valve to Sealing position. Press Pressure Cook or Manual; cook at high pressure 5 minutes.

3. When cooking is complete, use natural release for 10 minutes, then release remaining pressure.

4. Press Sauté; add corn and cornmeal to pot. Cook about 5 minutes or until chili thickens, stirring frequently. Stir in cilantro. Sprinkle each serving with 2 tablespoons cheese; garnish with green onions.

Makes 4 servings

PESTO TURKEY MEATBALLS

1 pound ground turkey

⅓ cup prepared pesto

⅓ cup grated Parmesan cheese,
plus additional for garnish

¼ cup panko bread crumbs

1 egg

2 green onions, finely chopped

½ teaspoon salt, divided

2 tablespoons olive oil

2 cloves garlic, minced

⅛ teaspoon red pepper flakes

1 can (28 ounces) whole tomatoes,
undrained, crushed with hands
or coarsely chopped

1 tablespoon tomato paste

Hot cooked pasta (optional)

1. Combine turkey, pesto, ⅓ cup cheese, panko, egg, green onions and ¼ teaspoon salt in medium bowl; mix well. Shape mixture into 24 balls (about 1¼ inches). Refrigerate meatballs while preparing sauce.

2. Press Sauté; heat oil in Instant Pot. Add garlic and red pepper flakes; cook and stir 1 minute. Add tomatoes with liquid, tomato paste and remaining ¼ teaspoon salt; cook 3 minutes or until sauce begins to simmer, stirring occasionally.

3. Remove about 1 cup sauce from pot. Arrange meatballs in single layer in pot; pour reserved sauce over meatballs.

4. Secure lid and move pressure release valve to Sealing position. Press Pressure Cook or Manual; cook at high pressure 10 minutes.

5. When cooking is complete, use natural release for 10 minutes, then release remaining pressure. If sauce is too thin, press Sauté and cook 5 minutes or until sauce thickens, stirring frequently. Serve over pasta, if desired. Garnish with additional cheese.

Makes 4 servings

SPANISH CHICKEN AND RICE

2 tablespoons olive oil

1 package (about 12 ounces) kielbasa
    sausage, cut into ½-inch slices

2 pounds boneless skinless chicken thighs
    (about 6)

1 onion, chopped

4 cloves garlic, minced

2 cups uncooked converted long grain rice

1 red bell pepper, diced

½ cup diced carrots

¾ teaspoon salt

¼ teaspoon black pepper

¼ teaspoon saffron threads (optional)

3 cups chicken broth

½ cup thawed frozen peas

1. Press Sauté; heat oil in Instant Pot. Add sausage; cook about 6 minutes or until browned. Remove to plate. Add chicken to pot in batches; cook about 8 minutes or until browned on both sides. Remove to plate.

2. Add onion to pot; cook and stir 3 minutes or until softened. Add garlic; cook and stir 30 seconds. Add rice, bell pepper, carrots, salt, black pepper and saffron, if desired; cook and stir 3 minutes. Stir in broth, scraping up browned bits from bottom of pot. Return chicken and sausage to pot, pressing chicken into liquid.

3. Secure lid and move pressure release valve to Sealing position. Press Pressure Cook or Manual; cook at high pressure 7 minutes.

4. When cooking is complete, press Cancel and use quick release. Remove chicken to clean plate; tent with foil.

5. Stir in peas; let stand 2 minutes or until peas are heated through. Serve chicken with rice mixture.

Makes 6 servings

MOROCCAN CHICKEN STEW

2 tablespoons olive oil, divided

1 pound boneless skinless chicken thighs, cut into 2-inch pieces

½ cup chopped onion

½ cup chopped celery

½ cup chopped carrots

3 cloves garlic, minced

½ teaspoon salt

½ teaspoon ground coriander

½ teaspoon ground cinnamon

¼ teaspoon dried oregano

⅛ teaspoon ground ginger

⅛ teaspoon black pepper

¾ cup dry white wine

⅓ cup chopped prunes

2 tablespoons white balsamic vinegar

1 tablespoon packed brown sugar

1 bay leaf

1. Press Sauté; heat 1 tablespoon oil in Instant Pot. Add chicken; cook and stir about 5 minutes or until no longer pink. Remove to plate.

2. Add remaining 1 tablespoon oil, onion, celery and carrots to pot; cook and stir 3 minutes or until vegetables are softened. Add garlic, salt, coriander, cinnamon, oregano, ginger and pepper; cook and stir 1 minute. Stir in wine, scraping up browned bits from bottom of pot. Stir in prunes, vinegar, brown sugar and bay leaf; mix well.

3. Secure lid and move pressure release valve to Sealing position. Press Pressure Cook or Manual; cook at high pressure 6 minutes.

4. When cooking is complete, use natural release for 10 minutes, then release remaining pressure. Remove and discard bay leaf.

Makes 2 to 3 servings

LAMB AND CHICKPEA STEW

1 cup dried chickpeas, soaked 8 hours or overnight

2 tablespoons vegetable oil, divided

1 pound lamb stew meat

1 large onion, chopped

1 tablespoon minced garlic

1½ teaspoons salt

1½ teaspoons ground cumin

1 teaspoon ground turmeric

1 teaspoon ground coriander

1 teaspoon ground cinnamon

¼ teaspoon black pepper

1 can (about 14 ounces) diced tomatoes

1½ cups chicken broth

½ cup chopped dried apricots, divided

¼ cup chopped fresh Italian parsley

2 tablespoons lemon juice

1 tablespoon honey

Hot cooked couscous (optional)

1. Drain and rinse chickpeas. Press Sauté; heat 1 tablespoon oil in Instant Pot. Add lamb; cook 6 minutes or until browned, stirring occasionally. Add remaining 1 tablespoon oil and onion to pot; cook and stir 3 minutes or until softened. Add garlic, salt, cumin, turmeric, coriander, cinnamon and pepper; cook and stir 1 minute. Add tomatoes and broth; cook and stir 2 minutes, scraping up browned bits from bottom of pot. Stir in chickpeas and half of apricots; mix well.

2. Secure lid and move pressure release valve to Sealing position. Press Pressure Cook or Manual; cook at high pressure 20 minutes.

3. When cooking is complete, use natural release for 10 minutes, then release remaining pressure.

4. Press Sauté; add remaining half of apricots to pot. Cook 5 minutes or until sauce is reduced and thickens slightly, stirring frequently. Stir in parsley, lemon juice and honey. Serve with couscous, if desired.

Makes 4 to 6 servings

BEEF POT ROAST DINNER

2 cloves garlic, minced

1 teaspoon salt

1 teaspoon herbes de Provence*

1 teaspoon ground sage

1 teaspoon ground cumin

1 teaspoon black pepper

1 beef eye of round roast (about 2½ pounds), well trimmed

2 tablespoons olive oil

¾ cup beef broth

4 small turnips, peeled and cut into wedges

12 medium fresh brussels sprouts, trimmed

2 cups halved small new red potatoes

2 cups baby carrots

1 cup pearl onions, skins removed *or* 1 large onion, cut into wedges

Or substitute ¼ teaspoon each dried rosemary, thyme, sage and savory.

1. Combine garlic, salt, herbes de Provence, sage, cumin and pepper in small bowl; mix well. Rub mixture into all sides of beef.

2. Press Sauté; heat oil in Instant Pot. Add beef; cook about 5 minutes or until browned on all sides. Remove to plate. Stir in broth, scraping up browned bits from bottom of pot. Place rack in pot; place beef on rack.

3. Secure lid and move pressure release valve to Sealing position. Press Pressure Cook or Manual; cook at high pressure 50 minutes.

4. When cooking is complete, use natural release for 5 minutes, then release remaining pressure.

5. Add turnips, brussels sprouts, potatoes, carrots and onions to pot. Secure lid and move pressure release valve to Sealing position. Press Pressure Cook or Manual; cook at high pressure 10 minutes.

6. When cooking is complete, press Cancel and use quick release. Serve beef and vegetables with cooking liquid or thicken sauce, if desired.

Makes 4 to 6 servings

IRISH BEEF STEW

2½ tablespoons vegetable oil, divided

2 pounds boneless beef chuck roast, cut into 1-inch pieces

1½ teaspoons salt, divided

¾ teaspoon black pepper, divided

1 package (8 to 10 ounces) cremini mushrooms, quartered

1 medium onion, quartered

1 cup Guinness stout

1 tablespoon Dijon mustard

1 tablespoon tomato paste

1 tablespoon Worcestershire sauce

2 cloves garlic, minced

2 bay leaves

1 teaspoon dried thyme

1 teaspoon dried rosemary

1 pound small yellow potatoes (about 1¼ inches), halved

3 medium carrots, cut into ¾-inch pieces

3 medium parsnips, cut into ¾-inch pieces

2 teaspoons water

2 teaspoons cornstarch

1 cup frozen pearl onions

Chopped fresh parsley (optional)

1. Press Sauté; heat 2 tablespoons oil in Instant Pot. Season beef with 1 teaspoon salt and ½ teaspoon pepper. Cook beef in two batches about 5 minutes or until browned. Remove to plate.

2. Add remaining ½ tablespoon oil, mushrooms and onion quarters to pot; cook about 6 minutes or until mushrooms give off their liquid and begin to brown, stirring frequently. Add Guinness, mustard, tomato paste, Worcestershire sauce, garlic, bay leaves, thyme, rosemary, remaining ½ teaspoon salt and ¼ teaspoon pepper; cook and stir 3 minutes, scraping up browned bits from bottom of pot. Return beef and any accumulated juices to pot; mix well.

3. Secure lid and move pressure release valve to Sealing position. Press Pressure Cook or Manual; cook at high pressure 30 minutes.

4. When cooking is complete, press Cancel and use quick release. Remove and discard bay leaves and large onion pieces. Add potatoes, carrots and parsnips to pot; mix well. Secure lid and move

pressure release valve to Sealing position. Press Pressure Cook or Manual; cook at high pressure 3 minutes. Meanwhile, stir water into cornstarch in small bowl until smooth.

5. When cooking is complete, press Cancel and use quick release. Press Sauté; stir pearl onions into stew. Add cornstarch mixture; cook 2 to 3 minutes or until stew thickens, stirring frequently. Garnish with parsley.

Makes 6 servings

CIDER PORK AND ONIONS

1 tablespoon vegetable oil

1 bone-in pork shoulder roast
   (4 to 4½ pounds)*

4 onions, cut into ¼-inch slices
   (about 4 cups)

1 cup apple cider, divided

1 teaspoon salt, divided

4 cloves garlic, minced

1 teaspoon dried rosemary

½ teaspoon black pepper

*A 4-pound roast requires a pressure cooker
that is 8 quarts or larger to fit.*

1. Press Sauté; heat oil in Instant Pot. Add pork; cook until browned on all sides. Remove to plate. Add onions, ¼ cup cider and ½ teaspoon salt to pot; cook 8 minutes or until onions are softened, scraping up browned bits from bottom of pot. Add garlic and rosemary, cook and stir 1 minute. Return pork to pot; sprinkle with remaining ½ teaspoon salt and pepper. Pour remaining ¾ cup cider over pork.

2. Secure lid and move pressure release valve to Sealing position. Press Pressure Cook or Manual; cook at high pressure 75 minutes.

3. When cooking is complete, use natural release. Remove pork to cutting board; tent with foil.

4. Meanwhile, press Sauté; cook 10 to 15 minutes or until sauce is reduced by one third. Skim fat from sauce; season with additional salt and pepper, if desired. Cut pork; serve with sauce.

Makes 8 servings

SOUTHWESTERN CHILE BEEF

2 **tablespoons vegetable oil, divided**

2 **pounds beef round roast, cut into bite-size pieces**

1 **onion, finely chopped**

2 **cloves garlic, minced**

1 **teaspoon all-purpose flour**

1 **teaspoon salt**

1 **teaspoon dried oregano**

½ **teaspoon ground cumin**

¼ **teaspoon black pepper**

5 **canned whole green chiles, chopped**

1 **canned chipotle pepper in adobo sauce, chopped**

Hot cooked polenta, rice or pasta (optional)

1. Press Sauté; heat 1 tablespoon oil in Instant Pot. Add half of beef; cook about 5 minutes or until browned, stirring occasionally. Remove to plate. Add remaining oil and beef; cook 3 minutes, stirring occasionally. Add onion and garlic; cook and stir 3 minutes or until beef is browned and onion is softened. Return first half of beef to pot. Add flour, salt, oregano, cumin and black pepper; cook and stir 30 seconds. Stir in green chiles and chipotle pepper; mix well.

2. Secure lid and move pressure release valve to Sealing position. Press Pressure Cook or Manual; cook at high pressure 35 minutes.

3. When cooking is complete, use natural release for 5 minutes, then release remaining pressure.

4. Press Sauté; cook 5 to 10 minutes or until sauce is reduced and thickens slightly. Serve over polenta, if desired.

Makes 4 servings

TRADITIONAL GOULASH

⅓ cup all-purpose flour

2½ teaspoons salt, divided

1 teaspoon black pepper

2 pounds boneless beef chuck shoulder, cut into bited-size pieces

3 tablespoons vegetable oil, divided

2 shallots *or* 1 medium onion, finely chopped

3 cloves garlic, minced

1 can (28 ounces) diced tomatoes

1 tablespoon paprika (preferably Hungarian)

2 tablespoons chopped fresh parsley *or* 1 teaspoon dried parsley flakes

1 teaspoon dried thyme

2 bay leaves

¼ cup sour cream, or to taste

Hot cooked egg noodles

Chopped fresh dill (optional)

1. Combine flour, 2 teaspoons salt and pepper in large resealable food storage bag. Add beef; shake to coat.

2. Press Sauté; heat 2 tablespoons oil in Instant Pot. Add beef in two batches; cook about 5 minutes or until browned. Remove to plate.

3. Heat remaining 1 tablespoon oil in pot. Add shallots and garlic; cook and stir 2 minutes or until softened. Add tomatoes and paprika; cook and stir 2 minutes, scraping up browned bits from bottom of pot. Return beef to pot with parsley, thyme, bay leaves and remaining ½ teaspoon salt; mix well.

4. Secure lid and move pressure release valve to Sealing position. Press Pressure Cook or Manual; cook at high pressure 35 minutes.

5. When cooking is complete, use natural release for 10 minutes, then release remaining pressure.

6. Press Sauté; cook 5 minutes or until stew thickens slightly. Turn off heat. Remove and discard bay leaves. Stir in sour cream until blended. Serve over noodles; garnish with dill.

Makes 4 to 6 servings

ONE-POT PASTA WITH SAUSAGE

1   tablespoon olive oil
1   pound smoked sausage (about 4 links),
        cut into ¼-inch slices
1   onion, diced
1   tablespoon tomato paste
2   cloves garlic, minced
1½ teaspoons dried oregano
¼   teaspoon red pepper flakes
1   can (28 ounces) whole tomatoes,
        undrained, crushed with hands
        or coarsely chopped

2½ cups water
1½ teaspoons salt
1   package (16 ounces) uncooked
        cellentani pasta
1½ cups frozen peas
½   cup shredded Parmesan cheese
⅓   cup shredded fresh basil leaves,
        plus additional for garnish

1. Press Sauté; heat oil in Instant Pot. Add sausage; cook about 7 minutes or until browned, stirring occasionally. Add onion; cook and stir 3 minutes or until softened. Add tomato paste, garlic, oregano and red pepper flakes; cook and stir 1 minute. Add tomatoes with liquid, water and salt; cook 2 minutes, scraping up browned bits from bottom of pot. Stir in pasta; mix well.

2. Secure lid and move pressure release valve to Sealing position. Press Pressure Cook or Manual; cook at high pressure 5 minutes.

3. When cooking is complete, use natural release for 5 minutes, then release remaining pressure.

4. Press Sauté; add peas to pot. Cook and stir 2 minutes. Turn off heat; stir in cheese and ⅓ cup basil. Cover pot with lid (do not lock) and let stand 2 minutes. Garnish with additional basil.

Makes 6 servings

VARIATION: You can substitute 1 pound uncooked Italian sausage (about 4 links) for the smoked sausage. Remove the casings, cut into ½-inch pieces and proceed with the recipe as directed.

TUSCAN BEEF STEW

¼ cup dried porcini mushrooms

½ cup hot water

3 slices bacon, chopped

1 tablespoon olive oil

2 pounds beef stew meat, cut into ½-inch pieces

1 teaspoon salt, divided

½ teaspoon black pepper, divided

3 cups assorted mushrooms (portobello, shiitake and/or cremini), sliced

2 cloves garlic, minced

1 teaspoon dried rosemary

1 can (about 14 ounces) diced tomatoes, drained

1 cup frozen pearl onions, thawed

1 cup baby carrots, cut into ½-inch pieces

¼ cup tomato paste

¼ cup dry red wine

2 tablespoons all-purpose flour

Hot cooked pasta (optional)

1. Place dried mushrooms in small bowl; cover with hot water. Let stand about 15 minutes or until softened. Meanwhile, press Sauté; cook bacon in Instant Pot until crisp. Remove to paper towel-lined plate. Drain off all but 1 tablespoon drippings. Add oil to pot. Season beef with ¼ teaspoon salt and ¼ teaspoon pepper; cook in two batches about 5 minutes or until browned. Remove to plate. Drain mushrooms; strain and reserve soaking liquid. Coarsely chop mushrooms.

2. Add chopped dried mushrooms, strained soaking liquid, sliced mushrooms, garlic and rosemary to pot; cook and stir 3 minutes, scraping up browned bits from bottom of pot. Stir in beef, tomatoes, onions, carrots, tomato paste, wine, remaining ¾ teaspoon salt and ¼ teaspoon pepper; mix well.

3. Secure lid and move pressure release valve to Sealing position. Press Pressure Cook or Manual; cook at high pressure 30 minutes. When cooking is complete, use natural release for 10 minutes, then release remaining pressure.

4. Place flour in small bowl; stir in ¼ cup hot liquid from pot until smooth. Press Sauté; add flour mixture to pot. Cook and stir about 3 minutes or until stew thickens. Serve over pasta, if desired.

Makes 6 to 8 servings

MAPLE SPICE RUBBED RIBS

3 teaspoons chili powder, divided

1¼ teaspoons ground coriander

1¼ teaspoons garlic powder, divided

¾ teaspoon salt

½ teaspoon black pepper

3 to 3½ pounds pork baby back ribs, trimmed and cut into 4-rib sections

4 tablespoons maple syrup, divided

1 can (8 ounces) tomato sauce

¼ teaspoon ground cinnamon

¼ teaspoon ground ginger

1. Combine 1½ teaspoons chili powder, coriander, ¾ teaspoon garlic powder, salt and pepper in small bowl; mix well. Brush ribs with 2 tablespoons maple syrup; rub with spice mixture. Place ribs in Instant Pot.

2. Combine tomato sauce, remaining 2 tablespoons maple syrup, 1½ teaspoons chili powder, ½ teaspoon garlic powder, cinnamon and ginger in medium bowl; mix well. Pour over ribs in pot; stir to coat ribs with sauce.

3. Secure lid and move pressure release valve to Sealing position. Press Pressure Cook or Manual; cook at high pressure 25 minutes.

4. When cooking is complete, use natural release for 10 minutes, then release remaining pressure. Remove ribs to plate; tent with foil.

5. Press Sauté; cook about 10 minutes or until sauce thickens. Brush ribs with sauce; serve remaining sauce on the side.

Makes 4 servings

BRISKET WITH VEGETABLES

1 tablespoon vegetable oil

1 beef brisket (4 to 5 pounds), well trimmed

2 onions, thinly sliced

4 cloves garlic, minced

2 teaspoons dried thyme

½ teaspoon ground coriander

¾ cup beef broth

1 teaspoon salt

½ teaspoon black pepper

2 pounds unpeeled red potatoes, quartered

1 pound baby carrots

3 tablespoons water

2 tablespoons all-purpose flour

1. Press Sauté; heat oil in Instant Pot. Add brisket; cook until browned on all sides. Remove to plate. Add onions to pot; cook and stir 3 minutes or until softened. Add garlic, thyme and coriander; cook and stir 1 minute. Add broth, salt and pepper; cook and stir 1 minute, scraping up browned bits from bottom of pot. Return brisket to pot.

2. Secure lid and move pressure release valve to Sealing position. Press Pressure Cook or Manual; cook at high pressure 60 minutes.

3. When cooking is complete, use natural release for 10 minutes, then release remaining pressure.

4. Add potatoes and carrots to pot. Secure lid and move pressure release valve to Sealing position. Press Pressure Cook or Manual; cook at high pressure 10 minutes. When cooking is complete, use natural release for 10 minutes, then release remaining pressure. Remove brisket and vegetables to platter; tent with foil.

5. Stir water into flour in small bowl until smooth. Add ¼ cup hot cooking liquid; stir until blended. Press Sauté; add flour mixture to remaining cooking liquid in pot. Cook and stir 3 to 4 minutes or until sauce thickens.

6. Slice brisket across the grain. Serve brisket and vegetables with sauce.

Makes 8 servings

TACO SALAD

CHILI

- 1 pound ground beef
- 1 medium onion, chopped
- 1 stalk celery, chopped
- 2 medium tomatoes, chopped
- 1 jalapeño pepper, finely chopped
- 1½ teaspoons chili powder
- 1 teaspoon salt
- 1 teaspoon ground cumin
- ½ teaspoon black pepper
- 1 can (15 ounces) tomato sauce
- 1 can (about 15 ounces) kidney beans, rinsed and drained
- 1 can (about 15 ounces) pinto beans, rinsed and drained
- ½ cup water

SALAD

- 8 cups chopped romaine lettuce
- 2 cups diced fresh tomatoes
- 2 cups small tortilla chips

  Optional toppings: salsa, sour cream, shredded Cheddar cheese

1. For chili, press Sauté; add beef to Instant Pot. Cook about 8 minutes or until browned, stirring frequently. Drain off fat and excess liquid. Add onion and celery to pot; cook and stir 3 minutes.

2. Add tomatoes, jalapeño, chili powder, salt, cumin and black pepper; cook and stir 1 minute. Stir in tomato sauce, beans and water; mix well.

3. Secure lid and move pressure release valve to Sealing position. Press Pressure Cook or Manual; cook at high pressure 20 minutes.

4. When cooking is complete, use natural release for 10 minutes, then release remaining pressure.

5. For each salad, combine 2 cups lettuce and ½ cup diced tomatoes in individual bowl. Top with tortilla chips, chili, salsa, sour cream and cheese, if desired. (Recipe makes more chili than needed for salads; reserve remaining chili for another use.)

Makes 4 servings

ITALIAN TOMATO-BRAISED LAMB

1 can (28 ounces) whole plum tomatoes, undrained

4 bone-in lamb shoulder chops (¾ to 1 inch thick, about 2 pounds)

1½ teaspoons dried oregano

½ teaspoon salt

¼ teaspoon black pepper

2 tablespoons olive oil

2 onions, cut into quarters and thinly sliced

3 cloves garlic, minced

2 tablespoons red wine vinegar

3 to 4 sprigs fresh rosemary

Hot cooked polenta or pasta (optional)

1. Drain tomatoes, reserving ¾ cup juice. Coarsely chop tomatoes. (Tomatoes can also be broken up with hands or cut with scissors in can.)

2. Season both sides of lamb with oregano, salt and pepper. Press Sauté; heat oil in Instant Pot. Add onions and garlic; cook and stir 3 minutes or until softened. Add tomatoes, reserved ¾ cup juice and vinegar; cook and stir 1 minute. Add lamb and rosemary to pot, pressing into liquid.

3. Secure lid and move pressure release valve to Sealing position. Press Pressure Cook or Manual; cook at high pressure 12 minutes.

4. When cooking is complete, use natural release for 10 minutes, then release remaining pressure. Remove lamb to plate; tent with foil. Remove and discard rosemary sprigs.

5. Press Sauté; cook 5 to 10 minutes or until sauce is reduced by one third. Serve sauce with lamb and polenta, if desired.

Makes 4 servings

GREEK BEEF STEW

¼ cup all-purpose flour

2 teaspoons Greek seasoning

¼ teaspoon salt

¼ teaspoon black pepper

2 pounds bottom round or boneless beef chuck roast, cut into 1-inch pieces

2 tablespoons olive oil

½ cup beef broth

¼ cup tomato paste

1 pint grape or cherry tomatoes, divided

2 medium onions, each cut into 8 wedges

1 cup pitted kalamata olives

4 sprigs fresh oregano, plus additional for garnish

1 lemon, divided

1. Combine flour, Greek seasoning, salt and pepper in large resealable food storage bag. Add beef; shake to coat.

2. Press Sauté; heat oil in Instant Pot. Cook beef in two batches about 5 minutes or until browned. Remove to plate. Add broth and tomato paste; cook and stir 2 minutes, scraping up browned bits from bottom of pot. Stir in beef, ½ cup grape tomatoes, onions, olives, 4 sprigs oregano and juice of ½ lemon; mix well.

3. Secure lid and move pressure release valve to Sealing position. Press Pressure Cook or Manual; cook at high pressure 20 minutes.

4. When cooking is complete, use natural release for 10 minutes, then release remaining pressure.

5. Press Sauté; add remaining grape tomatoes to pot. Cook about 5 minutes or until tomatoes have softened and stew thickens, stirring frequently. Cut remaining ½ lemon into wedges; serve with stew. Garnish with additional oregano.

Makes 4 to 6 servings

PORK PICADILLO

1 tablespoon olive oil

1 pound boneless pork country-style ribs, trimmed and cut into ½-inch pieces

1 onion, chopped

2 cloves garlic, minced

1 can (about 14 ounces) diced tomatoes

½ cup raisins

2 tablespoons cider vinegar

2 canned chipotle peppers in adobo sauce, chopped

½ teaspoon salt

½ teaspoon ground cumin

½ teaspoon ground cinnamon

1. Press Sauté; heat oil in Instant Pot. Add pork; cook about 6 minutes or until browned, stirring occasionally. Add onion; cook and stir 2 minutes. Add garlic; cook and stir 30 seconds. Stir in tomatoes, raisins, vinegar, chipotle peppers, salt, cumin and cinnamon, scraping up browned bits from bottom of pot.

2. Secure lid and move pressure release valve to Sealing position. Press Pressure Cook or Manual; cook at high pressure 25 minutes.

3. When cooking is complete, use natural release for 10 minutes, then release remaining pressure. Stir pork mixture with tongs, breaking up pork into smaller pieces.

Makes 4 servings

BEEF POT PIE

⅓ cup all-purpose flour

1½ teaspoons salt, divided

½ teaspoon black pepper, divided

1½ pounds beef stew meat, cut into 1-inch pieces

2 tablespoons olive oil

½ cup beef broth

⅓ cup stout, dark beer or ale

1 teaspoon chopped fresh thyme *or* ½ teaspoon dried thyme

1 pound unpeeled new red potatoes, cut into 1-inch pieces

2 cups baby carrots, halved crosswise

1 cup frozen pearl onions, thawed *or* 1 large onion, chopped

1 parsnip, peeled and cut into 1-inch pieces

1 refrigerated pie crust (half of 15-ounce package)

1. Combine flour, ½ teaspoon salt and ¼ teaspoon pepper in large resealable food storage bag. Add beef; toss to coat.

2. Press Sauté; heat oil in Instant Pot. Add beef in two batches; cook about 5 minutes or until browned. Stir in broth, stout, thyme, remaining 1 teaspoon salt and ¼ teaspoon pepper; mix well.

3. Secure lid and move pressure release valve to Sealing position. Press Pressure Cook or Manual; cook at high pressure 25 minutes.

4. When cooking is complete, press Cancel and use quick release. Add potatoes, carrots, onions and parsnip to pot; mix well. Secure lid and move pressure release valve to Sealing position. Press Pressure Cook or Manual; cook at high pressure 15 minutes. Meanwhile, remove pie crust from refrigerator; let stand at room temperature 15 minutes. Preheat oven to 425°F.

5. When cooking is complete, press Cancel and use quick release. Pour beef mixture into 2½- to 3-quart baking dish. Place pie crust over filling; press edges to seal. Cut slits in crust to vent.

6. Bake 15 to 20 minutes or until crust is golden brown. Cool slightly before serving.

Makes 4 to 6 servings

CANTON PORK STEW

1 cup chicken broth

¼ cup dry sherry

3 tablespoons soy sauce

1 tablespoon hoisin sauce

1½ tablespoons cornstarch

2 tablespoons vegetable oil

1½ pounds boneless pork shoulder, trimmed and cut into 1-inch pieces

1 large onion, chopped

3 cloves garlic, minced

1 teaspoon Chinese five-spice powder

½ teaspoon salt

2 cups baby carrots

1 large green bell pepper, cut into 1-inch pieces

1. Combine broth, sherry, soy sauce and hoisin sauce in medium bowl; mix well. Stir 3 tablespoons broth mixture into cornstarch in small bowl until smooth; set aside.

2. Press Sauté; heat oil in Instant Pot. Add pork in two batches; cook about 5 minutes or until browned. Remove to plate.

3. Add onion to pot; cook and stir 3 minutes or until softened. Add garlic, five-spice powder and salt; cook and stir 30 seconds. Add broth mixture; cook and stir 1 minute, scraping up browned bits from bottom of pot. Return pork to pot.

4. Secure lid and move pressure release valve to Sealing position. Press Pressure Cook or Manual; cook at high pressure 15 minutes.

5. When cooking is complete, press Cancel and use quick release. Add carrots and bell pepper to pot. Secure lid and move pressure release valve to Sealing position. Press Pressure Cook or Manual; cook at high pressure 2 minutes. When cooking is complete, press Cancel and use quick release.

6. Stir reserved cornstarch mixture. Press Sauté; add cornstarch mixture to pot, stirring constantly. Cook and stir about 1 minute or until stew thickens.

Makes 6 servings

ESPRESSO-LACED POT ROAST

1 tablespoon packed brown sugar

1 tablespoon espresso powder

1½ teaspoons salt, divided

1 teaspoon black pepper, divided

1 boneless beef chuck pot roast
(2 to 2½ pounds)

1½ tablespoons vegetable oil

1 large onion, chopped

1 cup beef broth

½ teaspoon dried thyme

2 bay leaves

6 to 8 red potatoes (about 2 pounds),
peeled and cut into 1-inch pieces

1 pound carrots, cut into 1-inch pieces

3 tablespoons water

2 tablespoons all-purpose flour

Chopped fresh parsley (optional)

1. Combine brown sugar, espresso powder, ½ teaspoon salt and ½ teaspoon pepper in small bowl; mix well. Rub mixture over all sides of beef.

2. Press Sauté; heat oil in Instant Pot. Add beef; cook about 6 minutes or until browned on all sides. Remove to plate. Add onion to pot; cook and stir 3 minutes or until softened. Add broth, thyme, bay leaves, remaining 1 teaspoon salt and ½ teaspoon pepper; cook and stir 2 minutes, scraping up browned bits from bottom of pot. Return beef to pot.

3. Secure lid and move pressure release valve to Sealing position. Press Pressure Cook or Manual; cook at high pressure 60 minutes. When cooking is complete, press Cancel and use quick release.

4. Add potatoes and carrots to pot, pressing vegetables into cooking liquid. Secure lid and move pressure release valve to Sealing position. Press Pressure Cook or Manual; cook at high pressure 4 minutes. When cooking is complete, press Cancel and use quick release. Remove beef and vegetables to platter; tent with foil. Remove and discard bay leaves.

5. Stir water into flour in small bowl until smooth. Press Sauté. Add flour mixture to sauce; cook about 5 minutes or until sauce is reduced and thickens, stirring frequently. Serve sauce with beef and vegetables; garnish with parsley.

Makes 4 to 6 servings

SIMPLE SLOPPY JOES

1½ pounds ground beef
1 red bell pepper, chopped
½ cup chopped onion
1 clove garlic, minced
¼ cup ketchup
¼ cup barbecue sauce
2 tablespoons cider vinegar

1 tablespoon Worcestershire sauce
1 tablespoon packed brown sugar
1 teaspoon chili powder
1 can (about 8 ounces) baked beans
6 sandwich rolls, split
¾ cup (3 ounces) shredded Cheddar cheese (optional)

1. Press Sauté; add beef to Instant Pot. Cook about 8 minutes or until browned, stirring frequently. Drain off fat and excess liquid. Add bell pepper, onion and garlic to pot; cook and stir 3 minutes. Add ketchup, barbecue sauce, vinegar, Worcestershire sauce, brown sugar and chili powder; mix well.

2. Secure lid and move pressure release valve to Sealing position. Press Pressure Cook or Manual; cook at high pressure 10 minutes.

3. When cooking is complete, press Cancel and use quick release.

4. Press Sauté; add beans to pot. Cook 5 minutes or until beef mixture thickens, stirring frequently.

5. Serve beef mixture on rolls; sprinkle with cheese, if desired.

Makes 6 servings

PORK ROAST WITH FRUIT

2 cups water

2 tablespoons salt

1 tablespoon sugar

1 teaspoon dried thyme

1 bay leaf

½ teaspoon black pepper

1 boneless pork loin roast (3 to 3½ pounds)

1 tablespoon olive oil

⅓ cup dry red wine

Juice of ½ lemon

2 cloves garlic, minced

2 cups green grapes

1 cup dried apricots

1 cup dried prunes

1. Combine water, salt, sugar, thyme, bay leaf and pepper in large resealable food storage bag. Add pork; seal bag and turn to coat. Refrigerate overnight or up to 2 days, turning occasionally.

2. Remove pork from brine; discard liquid. Pat dry with paper towels. Press Sauté; heat oil in Instant Pot. Add pork; cook about 10 minutes or until browned on all sides. Remove to plate. Add wine, lemon juice and garlic; cook and stir 1 minute, scraping up browned bits from bottom of pot. Add grapes, apricots and prunes; mix well. Return pork to pot.

3. Secure lid and move pressure release valve to Sealing position. Press Pressure Cook or Manual; cook at high pressure 20 minutes.

4. When cooking is complete, use natural release. Remove pork to cutting board; tent with foil and let stand 10 minutes.

5. Meanwhile, press Sauté; cook 10 minutes or until sauce is reduced and thickens slightly. Slice pork; serve with sauce.

Makes 8 servings

SEAFOOD

SAVORY COD STEW

8 ounces bacon, chopped

1 large onion, diced

1 large carrot, diced

2 stalks celery, diced

2 cloves garlic, minced

1 can (28 ounces) plum tomatoes, undrained, coarsely chopped

2 potatoes, peeled and diced

1 cup clam juice

3 tablespoons tomato paste

3 tablespoons chopped fresh Italian parsley

½ teaspoon salt

¼ teaspoon black pepper

3 saffron threads

2½ pounds fresh cod, skin removed, cut into 1½-inch pieces

1. Press Sauté; cook bacon in Instant Pot until crisp. Drain off all but 2 tablespoons drippings.

2. Add onion, carrot, celery and garlic to pot; cook and stir 5 minutes or until vegetables are softened. Add tomatoes with juice, potatoes, clam juice, tomato paste, parsley, salt, pepper and saffron; cook and stir 2 minutes.

3. Secure lid and move pressure release valve to Sealing position. Press Pressure Cook or Manual; cook at high pressure 2 minutes.

4. When cooking is complete, press Cancel and use quick release.

5. Add cod to pot. Secure lid and move pressure release valve to Sealing position. Press Pressure Cook or Manual; cook at low pressure 1 minute.

6. When cooking is complete, press Cancel and use quick release.

Makes 6 to 8 servings

GREEK-STYLE SALMON

1 tablespoon olive oil

1 can (about 14 ounces) diced tomatoes, drained

¼ cup pitted black olives, coarsely chopped

¼ cup pitted green olives, coarsely chopped

3 tablespoons lemon juice

2 tablespoons chopped fresh Italian parsley

1 tablespoon capers, rinsed and drained

2 cloves garlic, thinly sliced

¼ teaspoon black pepper

1 pound salmon fillets

1. Press Sauté; heat oil in Instant Pot. Add tomatoes, olives, lemon juice, parsley, capers, garlic and pepper; bring to a simmer, stirring frequently.

2. Secure lid and move pressure release valve to Sealing position. Press Pressure Cook or Manual; cook at high pressure 4 minutes.

3. When cooking is complete, press Cancel and use quick release.

4. Place salmon in pot, skin side down. Press Sauté; bring to a simmer. Turn off heat; cover pot with lid and let stand 10 minutes or until fish begins to flake when tested with fork.

Makes 4 servings

SHRIMP AND OKRA GUMBO

1 tablespoon olive oil

8 ounces kielbasa sausage, halved lengthwise then cut crosswise into ¼-inch slices

1 green bell pepper, chopped

1 medium onion, chopped

3 stalks celery, cut into ¼-inch slices

6 green onions, chopped

4 cloves garlic, minced

1 can (about 14 ounces) diced tomatoes

½ cup chicken broth

1 teaspoon Cajun seasoning

½ teaspoon dried thyme

¼ teaspoon salt

2 cups frozen cut okra, thawed

1 pound large raw shrimp, peeled and deveined (with tails on)

1. Press Sauté; heat oil in Instant Pot. Add kielbasa; cook and stir 4 minutes or until browned. Remove to plate.

2. Add bell pepper, chopped onion, celery, green onions and garlic to pot; cook and stir 6 minutes or until vegetables are softened. Stir in kielbasa, tomatoes, broth, Cajun seasoning, thyme and salt; mix well.

3. Secure lid and move pressure release valve to Sealing position. Press Pressure Cook or Manual; cook at high pressure 4 minutes.

4. When cooking is complete, press Cancel and use quick release.

5. Add okra to pot. Secure lid and move pressure release valve to Sealing position. Press Pressure Cook or Manual; cook at high pressure 1 minute. When cooking is complete, press Cancel and use quick release.

6. Press Sauté; add shrimp to pot. Cook 2 to 3 minutes or until shrimp are pink and opaque, stirring occasionally.

Makes 6 servings

SCALLOPS WITH HERB TOMATO SAUCE

2 tablespoons vegetable oil

1 medium red onion, peeled and diced

1 clove garlic, minced

3½ cups fresh tomatoes, peeled*

1 can (6 ounces) tomato paste

¼ cup dry red wine

2 tablespoons chopped fresh Italian parsley

1 tablespoon chopped fresh oregano

1 teaspoon salt

¼ teaspoon black pepper

1½ pounds fresh scallops, cleaned and drained

Hot cooked pasta or rice (optional)

*To peel tomatoes, score "x" in bottom of tomatoes and place one at a time in simmering water about 10 seconds. (Add 30 seconds if tomatoes are not fully ripened.) Immediately plunge into bowl of cold water for another 10 seconds. Peel skin with a knife.

1. Press Sauté; heat oil in Instant Pot. Add onion and garlic; cook and stir 3 to 4 minutes or until onion is soft and translucent. Add tomatoes, tomato paste, wine, parsley, oregano, 1 teaspoon salt and ¼ teaspoon pepper; mix well.

2. Secure lid and move pressure release valve to Sealing position. Press Pressure Cook or Manual; cook at high pressure 8 minutes.

3. When cooking is complete, press Cancel and use quick release. Taste sauce; season with additional salt and pepper if necessary.

4. Press Sauté; add scallops to pot. Cook 1 minute or until sauce begins to simmer. Press Cancel; cover pot with lid and let stand 8 minutes or until scallops are opaque. Serve with pasta, if desired.

Makes 4 servings

ITALIAN FISH SOUP

1   can (about 14 ounces) Italian-seasoned diced tomatoes

1   cup chicken broth

1   small bulb fennel, chopped (about 1 cup), fronds reserved for garnish

3   cloves garlic, minced

1   tablespoon olive oil

½   teaspoon saffron threads, crushed (optional)

½   teaspoon dried basil

¼   teaspoon salt

¼   teaspoon red pepper flakes

8   ounces skinless halibut or cod fillets, cut into 1-inch pieces

8   ounces medium raw shrimp, peeled and deveined

1. Combine tomatoes, broth, chopped fennel, garlic, oil, saffron, if desired, basil, salt and red pepper flakes in Instant Pot; mix well.

2. Secure lid and move pressure release valve to Sealing position. Press Pressure Cook or Manual; cook at high pressure 3 minutes. When cooking is complete, press Cancel and use quick release.

3. Add halibut to pot. Secure lid and move pressure release valve to Sealing position. Press Pressure Cook or Manual; cook at low pressure 1 minute.

4. When cooking is complete, press Cancel and use quick release.

5. Press Sauté; add shrimp to pot. Cook 2 to 3 minutes or until shrimp are pink and opaque, stirring occasionally. Garnish soup with fennel fronds.

Makes 4 servings

SEA BASS WITH VEGETABLES

2 tablespoons butter or olive oil

2 bulbs fennel, thinly sliced

3 large carrots, julienned

3 large leeks, thinly sliced

¾ teaspoon salt, divided

¼ teaspoon plus ⅛ teaspoon black pepper, divided

6 sea bass fillets or other firm-fleshed white fish (6 to 8 ounces each)

¼ cup water

1. Press Sauté; melt butter in Instant Pot. Add fennel, carrots and leeks; cook about 8 minutes or until vegetables are softened and beginning to brown, stirring occasionally. Stir in ½ teaspoon salt and ¼ teaspoon pepper. Remove half of vegetables to plate.

2. Season sea bass with remaining ¼ teaspoon salt and ⅛ teaspoon pepper; place on top of vegetables in pot. Top with remaining vegetables. Drizzle with water.

3. Secure lid and move pressure release valve to Sealing position. Press Pressure Cook or Manual; cook at low pressure 4 minutes.

4. When cooking is complete, press Cancel and use quick release. Serve sea bass with vegetables.

Makes 6 servings

COD CHOWDER

2 tablespoons vegetable oil

1 pound unpeeled red potatoes, diced

2 medium leeks, halved and thinly sliced

2 stalks celery, diced

1 bulb fennel, diced

½ yellow or red bell pepper, diced

2 teaspoons chopped fresh thyme

1¼ teaspoons salt

½ teaspoon black pepper

2 tablespoons all-purpose flour

2 cups clam juice

1 cup water

1½ pounds cod, cut into 1-inch pieces

1 cup frozen corn

1 cup half-and-half

¼ cup finely chopped fresh Italian parsley

1. Press Sauté; heat oil in Instant Pot. Add potatoes, leeks, celery, fennel, bell pepper, thyme, salt and black pepper; cook about 8 minutes or until vegetables are slightly softened, stirring occasionally. Add flour; cook and stir 1 minute. Add clam juice and water; mix well.

2. Secure lid and move pressure release valve to Sealing position. Press Pressure Cook or Manual; cook at high pressure 6 minutes.

3. When cooking is complete, press Cancel and use quick release. Use immersion blender to blend soup just until slightly thickened but still chunky (soup should not be completely smooth).

4. Press Sauté; add cod, corn, half-and-half and parsley to pot. Cook about 2 minutes or until soup begins to simmer and fish is firm and opaque, stirring occasionally.

Makes 6 to 8 servings

MISO SALMON

½ cup water

2 green onions, cut into 2-inch pieces

¼ cup yellow miso paste

¼ cup soy sauce

2 tablespoons sake

2 tablespoons mirin

1½ teaspoons grated fresh ginger

1 teaspoon minced garlic

6 salmon fillets (about 4 ounces each)

Hot cooked rice (optional)

Thinly sliced green onions (optional)

1. Combine water, 2 green onions, miso, soy sauce, sake, mirin, ginger and garlic in Instant Pot; mix well. Add salmon to pot, skin side down.

2. Secure lid and move pressure release valve to Sealing position. Press Pressure Cook or Manual; cook at low pressure 4 minutes.

3. When cooking is complete, press Cancel and use quick release. Serve salmon with rice, if desired. Garnish with sliced green onions; drizzle with cooking liquid.

Makes 6 servings

TORTILLA SOUP WITH GROUPER

1	tablespoon vegetable oil	1	teaspoon salt
1	onion, chopped	1	teaspoon chili powder
2	cloves garlic, minced	1	teaspoon ground cumin
3½	cups chicken broth	⅛	teaspoon black pepper
1	can (about 14 ounces) diced tomatoes	1	pound grouper or sole fillets, cut into 1-inch pieces
1	can (4 ounces) diced green chiles, drained	1	cup frozen corn
2	teaspoons Worcestershire sauce	3	corn tortillas, cut into 1-inch strips

1. Press Sauté; heat oil in Instant Pot. Add onion and garlic; cook and stir 3 minutes or until onion is softened. Add broth, tomatoes, chiles, Worcestershire sauce, salt, chili powder, cumin and pepper; mix well.

2. Secure lid and move pressure release valve to Sealing position. Press Pressure Cook or Manual; cook at high pressure 4 minutes.

3. When cooking is complete, press Cancel and use quick release.

4. Press Sauté; add grouper and corn to pot. Cook about 2 minutes or until fish begins to flake when tested with fork. Stir in tortillas; serve immediately.

Makes 6 servings

CREAMY CRAB CHOWDER

1 tablespoon butter

1 cup finely chopped onion

2 cloves garlic, minced

1 cup chopped celery

½ cup chopped green bell pepper

½ cup chopped red bell pepper

3 cans (about 14 ounces each) chicken broth

3 cups diced peeled russet potatoes

1 teaspoon salt

½ teaspoon dried thyme

½ teaspoon black pepper

⅛ teaspoon ground red pepper

2 cans (6½ ounces each) lump crabmeat, drained and flaked

1 package (10 ounces) frozen corn

½ cup half-and-half

1. Press Sauté; melt butter in Instant Pot. Add onion and garlic; cook and stir 3 minutes or until softened. Add celery and bell peppers; cook and stir 4 minutes or until vegetables begin to soften. Stir in broth, potatoes, salt, thyme, black pepper and ground red pepper; mix well.

2. Secure lid and move pressure release valve to Sealing position. Press Pressure Cook or Manual; cook at high pressure 6 minutes.

3. When cooking is complete, press Cancel and use quick release.

4. Press Sauté; add crabmeat, corn and half-and-half to pot. Cook and stir 2 minutes or until soup begins to simmer.

Makes 6 to 8 servings

QUICK SHRIMP AND OKRA STEW

1 teaspoon vegetable oil

½ cup finely chopped onion

8 ounces okra, ends trimmed, cut into
   ½-inch slices

1 can (about 14 ounces) whole tomatoes,
   undrained, chopped

1 teaspoon dried thyme

¾ teaspoon salt

8 ounces medium raw shrimp, peeled
   and deveined

¾ cup fresh corn kernels or thawed
   frozen corn

½ teaspoon hot pepper sauce

1. Press Sauté; heat oil in Instant Pot. Add onion; cook and stir 3 minutes or until softened. Add okra; cook and stir 3 minutes. Add tomatoes with juice, thyme and salt; mix well.

2. Secure lid and move pressure release valve to Sealing position. Press Pressure Cook or Manual; cook at high pressure 4 minutes.

3. When cooking is complete, press Cancel and use quick release.

4. Press Sauté; add shrimp, corn and hot pepper sauce to pot. Cook 3 minutes or until shrimp are pink and opaque, stirring frequently.

Makes 4 servings

COD WITH TAPENADE

Tapenade (recipe follows)

4 cod fillets or other firm white fish
(about 8 ounces each)

¼ teaspoon salt

⅛ teaspoon black pepper

1 cup water

2 lemons, thinly sliced

1. Prepare Tapenade.

2. Season cod with salt and pepper. Pour water into Instant Pot. Place rack in pot; arrange half of lemon slices on rack. Place cod on lemon slices; top with remaining lemon slices.

3. Secure lid and move pressure release valve to Sealing position. Press Pressure Cook or Manual; cook at low pressure 2 minutes.

4. When cooking is complete, press Cancel and use quick release. Remove fish to serving plates; discard lemon slices. Serve with Tapenade.

Makes 4 servings

TAPENADE

8 ounces pitted kalamata olives

2 tablespoons anchovy paste

2 tablespoons drained capers

2 tablespoons chopped fresh Italian
parsley

1 clove garlic

½ teaspoon grated orange peel

⅛ teaspoon ground red pepper

½ cup extra virgin olive oil

Combine olives, anchovy paste, capers, parsley, garlic, orange peel and red pepper in food processor; pulse until coarsely chopped. Add oil; pulse until mixture forms rough paste. (Tapenade should not be completely smooth.)

Makes about 1 cup

LEMON–MINT RED POTATOES

2 pounds unpeeled new red potatoes
(1½ to 2 inches)

⅓ cup water

4 tablespoons chopped fresh mint, divided

1 tablespoon olive oil

1 teaspoon salt

1 teaspoon grated lemon peel

¾ teaspoon Greek seasoning or dried oregano

¼ teaspoon black pepper

1 tablespoon lemon juice

1 tablespoon butter

1. Combine potatoes, water, 2 tablespoons mint, oil, salt, lemon peel, Greek seasoning and pepper in Instant Pot; mix well.

2. Secure lid and move pressure release valve to Sealing position. Press Pressure Cook or Manual; cook at high pressure 6 minutes.

3. When cooking is complete, press Cancel and use quick release.

4. Press Sauté; add remaining 2 tablespoons mint, lemon juice and butter to pot. Cook and stir 2 minutes or until butter is melted and potatoes are completely coated.

Makes 4 servings

BALSAMIC GREEN BEANS WITH ALMONDS

1   cup water

1   pound fresh green beans, trimmed

1   tablespoon extra virgin olive oil

2   teaspoons balsamic vinegar

½   teaspoon salt

¼   teaspoon black pepper

2   tablespoons sliced almonds, toasted*

To toast almonds, cook in small skillet over medium heat 1 to 2 minutes or until lightly browned, stirring frequently.

1. Pour water into Instant Pot. Place rack in pot; place beans on rack. (Arrange beans perpendicular to rack to prevent beans from falling through.)

2. Secure lid and move pressure release valve to Sealing position. Press Pressure Cook or Manual; cook at high pressure 2 minutes.

3. When cooking is complete, press Cancel and use quick release. Remove rack from pot; place beans in large bowl.

4. Add oil, vinegar, salt and pepper; toss to coat. Sprinkle with almonds just before serving.

Makes 4 servings

CORN AND SWEET POTATO CURRY

1 tablespoon vegetable oil

1 large onion, chopped

2 tablespoons minced fresh ginger

½ jalapeño pepper, seeded and minced

2 cloves garlic, minced

1 cup frozen corn

2 teaspoons curry powder

½ teaspoon salt

1 can (about 13 ounces) coconut milk, well shaken

1 tablespoon soy sauce

4 sweet potatoes, peeled and cut into ¾-inch cubes

Hot cooked jasmine or long grain rice

Optional toppings: chopped fresh cilantro, finely chopped green onions, chopped peanuts

1. Press Sauté; heat oil in Instant Pot. Add onion, ginger, jalapeño and garlic; cook and stir 3 minutes or until softened. Add corn, curry powder and salt; cook and stir 1 minute. Add coconut milk and soy sauce; stir until well blended. Stir in sweet potatoes; mix well.

2. Secure lid and move pressure release valve to Sealing position. Press Pressure Cook or Manual; cook at high pressure 3 minutes.

3. When cooking is complete, press Cancel and use quick release.

4. Press Sauté; cook about 2 minutes or until thickened to desired consistency. Serve over rice; garnish with cilantro, green onions and peanuts.

Makes 6 servings

BRUSSELS SPROUTS IN ORANGE SAUCE

½ **cup plus 2 tablespoons orange juice, divided**

½ **teaspoon salt**

¼ **teaspoon red pepper flakes**

¼ **teaspoon ground cinnamon**

¼ **teaspoon black pepper**

8 **ounces fresh brussels sprouts (about 3 cups)**

2 **teaspoons cornstarch**

1 **teaspoon honey**

1 **teaspoon shredded or grated orange peel**

1. Combine ½ cup orange juice, salt, red pepper flakes, cinnamon and black pepper in Instant Pot; mix well. Stir in brussels sprouts.

2. Secure lid and move pressure release valve to Sealing position. Press Pressure Cook or Manual; cook at high pressure 2 minutes.

3. When cooking is complete, press Cancel and use quick release. Remove brussels sprouts to medium bowl with slotted spoon.

4. Stir remaining 2 tablespoons orange juice into cornstarch in small bowl until smooth. Press Sauté; add honey, orange peel and cornstarch mixture to pot. Cook 1 to 2 minutes or until sauce thickens, stirring constantly.

5. Pour sauce over brussels sprouts; stir gently to coat.

Makes 4 servings

WARM POTATO SALAD

2 **pounds fingerling potatoes**

¾ **cup water**

3 **slices thick-cut bacon, cut into
½-inch pieces**

1 **small onion, diced**

2 **tablespoons olive oil**

¼ **cup cider vinegar**

2 **tablespoons capers, drained and rinsed**

1 **tablespoon Dijon mustard**

¾ **teaspoon salt**

¼ **teaspoon black pepper**

⅓ **cup chopped fresh parsley**

1. Combine potatoes and water in Instant Pot. Secure lid and move pressure release valve to Sealing position. Press Pressure Cook or Manual; cook at high pressure 4 minutes.

2. When cooking is complete, press Cancel and use quick release. Drain potatoes; let stand until cool enough to handle. Dry out pot with paper towels.

3. Press Sauté; cook bacon in pot until crisp. Drain on paper towel-lined plate. Drain off all but 1 tablespoon drippings from pot. Adjust heat to low ("less"). Add onion and oil to pot; cook about 10 minutes or until onion begins to turn golden, stirring occasionally. Meanwhile, cut potatoes crosswise into ½-inch slices.

4. Add vinegar, capers, mustard, salt and pepper to pot; mix well. Turn off heat; stir in potatoes. Add parsley and bacon; stir gently to coat.

Makes 6 to 8 servings

SPEEDY MINESTRONE

1 tablespoon olive oil

1 medium onion, chopped

3 medium carrots, chopped

3 stalks celery, chopped

2 cloves garlic, minced

1½ teaspoons salt

1 teaspoon Italian seasoning

¼ teaspoon black pepper

⅛ teaspoon red pepper flakes

2 russet potatoes (about 6 ounces each), peeled and cut into ½-inch pieces

4 cups vegetable broth

2 cans (about 15 ounces each) cannellini beans, rinsed and drained

1 can (about 14 ounces) diced tomatoes

1 bunch kale, stemmed and chopped (about 6 cups)

Shredded Parmesan cheese (optional)

1. Press Sauté; heat oil in Instant Pot. Add onion, carrots, celery and garlic; cook and stir 5 minutes or until vegetables are softened. Add salt, Italian seasoning, black pepper and red pepper flakes; cook and stir 1 minute. Stir in potatoes, broth, beans and tomatoes; mix well.

2. Secure lid and move pressure release valve to Sealing position. Press Pressure Cook or Manual; cook at high pressure 3 minutes.

3. When cooking is complete, press Cancel and use quick release. Stir in kale. Secure lid and move pressure release valve to Sealing position. Press Pressure Cook or Manual; cook at high pressure 2 minutes.

4. When cooking is complete, use natural release for 5 minutes, then release remaining pressure. Serve with cheese, if desired.

Makes 6 to 8 servings

PARMESAN POTATO WEDGES

2　pounds unpeeled red potatoes (about
　　6 medium), cut into ½-inch wedges

½　cup water

¼　cup finely chopped onion

2　tablespoons butter, cut into small pieces

1¼　teaspoons salt

1　teaspoon dried oregano

¼　teaspoon black pepper

¼　cup grated Parmesan cheese

1. Combine potatoes, water, onion, butter, salt, oregano and pepper in Instant Pot; mix well.

2. Secure lid and move pressure release valve to Sealing position. Press Pressure Cook or Manual; cook at high pressure 3 minutes.

3. When cooking is complete, press Cancel and use quick release.

4. Transfer potatoes to serving platter; sprinkle with cheese.

Makes 4 to 6 servings

SHAKSHUKA

2 tablespoons extra virgin olive oil

1 large red bell pepper, chopped

1 medium onion, chopped

3 cloves garlic, minced

2 teaspoons sugar

2 teaspoons ground cumin

1 teaspoon paprika

1 teaspoon chili powder

½ teaspoon salt

¼ teaspoon red pepper flakes

1 can (28 ounces) crushed tomatoes

¾ cup crumbled feta cheese

4 eggs

1. Press Sauté; heat oil in Instant Pot. Add bell pepper and onion; cook and stir 3 minutes or until softened. Add garlic, sugar, cumin, paprika, chili powder, salt and red pepper flakes to pot; cook and stir 1 minute. Stir in tomatoes; mix well.

2. Secure lid and move pressure release valve to Sealing position. Press Pressure Cook or Manual; cook at high pressure 10 minutes.

3. When cooking is complete, press Cancel and use quick release.

4. Stir in cheese. Make four wells in sauce for eggs, leaving space between each. Slide eggs, one at a time, into wells in sauce. (For best results, crack each egg into small bowl before sliding into sauce.)

5. Secure lid and move pressure release valve to Sealing position. Press Pressure Cook or Manual; cook at low pressure 1 minute. When cooking is complete, press Cancel and use quick release. To cook eggs longer, press Sauté and cook until desired doneness.

Makes 4 servings

CARIBBEAN SWEET POTATOES

2½ **pounds sweet potatoes, peeled and cut into 1-inch pieces**

8 **ounces shredded peeled carrots**

¾ **cup flaked coconut, divided**

½ **cup water**

¼ **cup (½ stick) butter, cut into pieces**

2 **tablespoons sugar**

1 **teaspoon salt**

½ **cup chopped walnuts, toasted***

2 **tablespoons lime juice**

1 **teaspoon grated lime peel**

*To toast walnuts, cook in small skillet over medium heat 4 to 6 minutes or until fragrant, stirring frequently.

1. Combine sweet potatoes, carrots, ½ cup coconut, water, butter, sugar and salt in Instant Pot; mix well.

2. Secure lid and move pressure release valve to Sealing position. Press Pressure Cook or Manual; cook at high pressure 5 minutes.

3. Meanwhile, place remaining ¼ cup coconut in small skillet; cook 4 minutes or until lightly browned, stirring frequently.

4. When cooking is complete, press Cancel and use quick release.

5. Mash sweet potatoes in pot until desired consistency. Stir in walnuts, lime juice and lime peel until blended. Sprinkle with toasted coconut.

Makes 6 to 8 servings

SUMMER SQUASH LASAGNA

2   tablespoons olive oil

1   onion, chopped

1   medium zucchini, cut crosswise into ¼-inch slices

1   medium yellow squash, cut crosswise into ¼-inch slices

2   cloves garlic, minced

1   teaspoon salt, divided

1   cup ricotta cheese

1½ cups (6 ounces) shredded mozzarella cheese, divided

½   cup grated Parmesan cheese, divided

¼   cup plus 2 tablespoons chopped fresh basil, divided

1   egg

¼   teaspoon black pepper

2¼ cups marinara sauce

8   oven-ready (no-boil) lasagna noodles

1   cup water

1. Spray 7-inch springform pan with nonstick cooking spray. Heat oil in large skillet over medium-high heat. Add onion, zucchini and yellow squash; cook and stir about 5 minutes or until vegetables are softened and lightly browned. Add garlic and ½ teaspoon salt; cook and stir 30 seconds.

2. Combine ricotta, ¼ cup mozzarella, ¼ cup Parmesan, ¼ cup basil, egg, remaining ½ teaspoon salt and pepper in medium bowl; mix well.

3. Spread ¼ cup marinara sauce in bottom of prepared springform pan. Layer with 2 noodles, breaking to fit. Spread one third of ricotta mixture over noodles. Top with one third of vegetables, ¼ cup mozzarella and ½ cup sauce. Repeat layers twice. For final layer, top with remaining 2 noodles, ½ cup sauce, ½ cup mozzarella and ¼ cup Parmesan. Cover pan tightly with foil.

4. Pour water into Instant Pot. Place pan on rack; lower rack into pot. Secure lid and move pressure release valve to Sealing position. Press Pressure Cook or Manual; cook at high pressure 20 minutes.

5. When cooking is complete, use natural release. Carefully remove pan from pot. Remove foil.

6. If desired, preheat broiler and broil lasagna for 1 minute or until cheese is browned. Cool in pan 10 minutes. Remove side of pan; cut into squares or wedges. Sprinkle with remaining 2 tablespoons basil.

Makes 4 to 6 servings

LEMON PARMESAN CAULIFLOWER

1 cup water

3 tablespoons chopped fresh parsley

½ teaspoon grated lemon peel

1 large head cauliflower (2 to 3 pounds), trimmed

1 tablespoon butter

3 cloves garlic, minced

2 tablespoons lemon juice

½ teaspoon salt

¼ cup grated Parmesan cheese

1. Pour water into Instant Pot; stir in parsley and lemon peel. Place rack in pot; place cauliflower on rack.

2. Secure lid and move pressure release valve to Sealing position. Press Pressure Cook or Manual; cook at high pressure 3 minutes.

3. When cooking is complete, press Cancel and use quick release. Remove rack from pot; place cauliflower in large bowl. Reserve ½ cup cooking liquid; discard remaining liquid.

4. Press Sauté; melt butter in pot. Add garlic; cook and stir 1 minute or until fragrant. Add lemon juice, salt and reserved ½ cup cooking liquid; cook and stir until heated through.

5. Spoon lemon sauce over cauliflower; sprinkle with cheese. Cut into wedges to serve.

Makes 6 servings

SWEET POTATO AND BLACK BEAN CHILI

1 tablespoon olive oil

1 large onion, chopped

4 teaspoons chili powder

2 cloves garlic, minced

1 teaspoon salt

1 teaspoon chipotle chili powder

½ teaspoon ground cumin

2 cans (about 15 ounces each) black beans, rinsed and drained

1 large sweet potato, peeled and cut into ½-inch pieces

1 can (about 14 ounces) diced tomatoes

1 can (about 14 ounces) crushed tomatoes

1½ cups vegetable broth or water

Optional toppings: sour cream, sliced green onions, shredded Cheddar cheese and/or tortilla chips

1. Press Sauté; heat oil in Instant Pot. Add onion; cook and stir 3 minutes or until softened. Add chili powder, garlic, salt, chili powder and cumin; cook and stir 1 minute. Add beans, sweet potato, diced tomatoes, crushed tomatoes and broth; mix well.

2. Secure lid and move pressure release valve to Sealing position. Press Pressure Cook or Manual; cook at high pressure 4 minutes.

3. When cooking is complete, press Cancel and use quick release.

4. Press Sauté; cook and stir 3 to 5 minutes or until chili thickens to desired consistency. Serve with desired toppings.

Makes 6 servings

COCONUT BUTTERNUT SQUASH

1 tablespoon butter

½ cup chopped onion

1 butternut squash (about 3 pounds), peeled and cut into 1-inch pieces

1 can (about 13 ounces) coconut milk, well shaken

1 to 2 tablespoons packed brown sugar, divided

1¼ teaspoons salt

½ teaspoon ground cinnamon

¼ teaspoon ground nutmeg

¼ teaspoon ground allspice

2 teaspoons grated fresh ginger

2 tablespoons lemon juice

1. Press Sauté; melt butter in Instant Pot. Add onion; cook and stir 2 minutes. Add squash, coconut milk, 1 tablespoon brown sugar, salt, cinnamon, nutmeg and allspice; mix well.

2. Secure lid and move pressure release valve to Sealing position. Press Pressure Cook or Manual; cook at high pressure 6 minutes.

3. When cooking is complete, press Cancel and use quick release.

4. Stir ginger into squash mixture. Use immersion blender to blend squash until smooth (or process in food processor or blender). Stir in lemon juice. Sprinkle individual servings with remaining 1 tablespoon brown sugar, if desired.

Makes 4 to 6 servings

QUICK VEGETABLE CURRY

2 **teaspoons salt**

2 **teaspoons curry powder**

1 **teaspoon cumin seeds**

1 **teaspoon ground coriander**

¼ **teaspoon ground turmeric**

¼ **teaspoon ground red pepper**

1 **tablespoon vegetable oil**

1 **large onion, finely chopped**

4 **cloves garlic, minced**

1 **tablespoon grated fresh ginger**

¼ **cup tomato paste**

1 **cup water**

1 **head cauliflower (about 1 pound), broken into florets**

2 **baking potatoes, peeled and cut into ½-inch pieces**

1 **red bell pepper, cut into ½-inch pieces**

2 **carrots, cut into ¼-inch pieces**

1 **package (12 ounces) frozen peas, thawed**

1. Combine salt, curry powder, cumin seeds, coriander, turmeric and ground red pepper in small bowl; mix well.

2. Press Sauté; heat oil in Instant Pot. Add onion; cook and stir 3 minutes or until softened. Add garlic, ginger and spice mixture; cook and stir 1 minute. Add tomato paste; cook and stir 30 seconds. Stir in water, scraping up browned bits from bottom of pot. Add cauliflower, potatoes, bell pepper and carrots; stir to coat with sauce.

3. Secure lid and move pressure release valve to Sealing position. Press Pressure Cook or Manual; cook at high pressure 2 minutes.

4. When cooking is complete, press Cancel and use quick release.

5. Stir in peas; let stand 2 to 3 minutes or until heated through.

Makes 6 to 8 servings

CHUNKY RANCH POTATOES

3   pounds unpeeled red potatoes,
       quartered
½   cup water
1   teaspoon salt

½   cup ranch dressing
½   cup grated Parmesan cheese
¼   cup minced fresh chives

1. Combine potatoes, water and salt in Instant Pot; mix well.

2. Secure lid and move pressure release valve to Sealing position. Press Pressure Cook or Manual; cook at high pressure 5 minutes.

3. When cooking is complete, press Cancel and use quick release.

4. Add ranch dressing, cheese and chives to pot; stir gently to coat, breaking potatoes into chunks.

Makes 8 servings

MEDITERRANEAN STEW

1 tablespoon olive oil

1 onion, chopped

1 clove garlic, minced

1 teaspoon salt

½ teaspoon ground turmeric

½ teaspoon ground cumin

¼ teaspoon ground red pepper

¼ teaspoon paprika

¼ teaspoon ground cinnamon

1 medium butternut squash, peeled and cut into 1-inch cubes

1 medium eggplant, cut into 1-inch cubes (about 4 cups)

1 can (about 15 ounces) chickpeas, rinsed and drained

1 can (about 14 ounces) vegetable broth

1 package (10 ounces) frozen cut okra

1 can (8 ounces) tomato sauce

1 medium carrot, sliced

1 medium tomato, chopped

⅓ cup raisins

2 cups sliced zucchini

Hot cooked couscous or rice

Chopped fresh parsley (optional)

1. Press Sauté; heat oil in Instant Pot. Add onion; cook and stir 3 minutes or until softened. Add garlic, salt, turmeric, cumin, red pepper, paprika and cinnamon; cook and stir 30 seconds. Add butternut squash, eggplant, chickpeas, broth, okra, tomato sauce, carrot, tomato and raisins; mix well.

2. Secure lid and move pressure release valve to Sealing position. Press Pressure Cook or Manual; cook at high pressure 5 minutes.

3. When cooking is complete, press Cancel and use quick release.

4. Press Sauté; add zucchini to pot. Cook 3 minutes or until zucchini is tender, stirring occasionally. Serve over couscous; garnish with parsley.

Makes 6 servings

SOUTHWESTERN CORN AND BEANS

2 cups dried kidney beans, soaked 8 hours or overnight

1 tablespoon olive oil

1 large onion, chopped

1 jalapeño pepper, minced

1 clove garlic, minced

2 teaspoons chili powder

½ teaspoon ground cumin

1 can (about 14 ounces) diced tomatoes

1 green bell pepper, cut into 1-inch pieces

½ cup water

1½ teaspoons salt

½ teaspoon black pepper

1 package (16 ounces) frozen corn, thawed

1. Drain and rinse beans. Press Sauté; heat oil in Instant Pot. Add onion; cook and stir 3 minutes or until softened. Add jalapeño, garlic, chili powder and cumin; cook and stir 1 minute. Add tomatoes, bell pepper, water, salt and black pepper; mix well. Stir in beans.

2. Secure lid and move pressure release valve to Sealing position. Press Pressure Cook or Manual; cook at high pressure 25 minutes.

3. When cooking is complete, use natural release for 10 minutes, then release remaining pressure.

4. Press Sauté; stir in corn. Cook about 5 minutes or until mixture thickens and corn is heated through, stirring occasionally.

Makes 6 servings

MASHED ROOT VEGETABLES

1 **pound baking potatoes, peeled and cut into 1-inch pieces**

1 **pound turnips, peeled and cut into 1-inch pieces**

12 **ounces sweet potatoes, peeled and cut into 1-inch pieces**

8 **ounces parsnips, peeled and cut into ½-inch pieces**

¼ **cup (½ stick) butter, cubed**

⅓ **cup water**

2 **teaspoons salt**

¼ **teaspoon black pepper**

½ **cup milk**

1. Combine baking potatoes, turnips, sweet potatoes, parsnips, butter, water, salt and pepper in Instant Pot; mix well.

2. Secure lid and move pressure release valve to Sealing position. Press Pressure Cook or Manual; cook at high pressure 10 minutes.

3. When cooking is complete, press Cancel and use quick release.

4. Mash vegetables with potato masher until almost smooth. Press Sauté; stir in milk until blended. Cook and stir about 3 minutes or until milk is absorbed and vegetables reach desired consistency.

Makes 6 servings

FARRO RISOTTO WITH MUSHROOMS AND SPINACH

2	tablespoons olive oil, divided	2	cloves garlic, minced
1	onion, chopped	1	cup uncooked pearled farro
12	ounces cremini mushrooms, trimmed and quartered	1	sprig fresh thyme
1	teaspoon salt	1½	cups vegetable or chicken broth
¼	teaspoon black pepper	1	package (5 to 6 ounces) baby spinach
		½	cup grated Parmesan cheese

1. Press Sauté; heat 1 tablespoon oil in Instant Pot. Add onion; cook and stir 5 minutes or until translucent. Add remaining 1 tablespoon oil, mushrooms, salt and pepper; cook about 8 minutes or until mushrooms have released their liquid and are browned, stirring occasionally. Add garlic; cook and stir 1 minute. Add farro and thyme; cook and stir 1 minute. Add broth; mix well.

2. Secure lid and move pressure release valve to Sealing position. Press Pressure Cook or Manual; cook at high pressure 10 minutes.

3. When cooking is complete, use natural release for 10 minutes, then release remaining pressure. Remove and discard thyme sprig.

4. Stir in spinach and cheese until spinach is wilted.

Makes 4 servings

MUSHROOM AND CHICKPEA RAGOÛT

1 cup dried chickpeas, soaked 8 hours or overnight

3 tablespoons olive oil

8 ounces sliced cremini mushrooms

8 ounces shiitake mushrooms,* stemmed and thinly sliced

1 onion, chopped

4 cloves garlic, minced

½ cup Madeira wine

2 teaspoons salt

1 teaspoon dried rosemary

Black pepper

1 can (28 ounces) crushed tomatoes

1 cup water

1 can (6 ounces) tomato paste

Polenta (recipe follows, optional)

Or substitute an additional 8 ounces of cremini mushrooms for the shiitake mushrooms.

1. Drain and rinse chickpeas. Press Sauté; heat oil in Instant Pot. Add mushrooms, onion and garlic; cook and stir 6 minutes or until mushrooms are browned. Add Madeira, salt and rosemary; cook and stir 1 to 2 minutes or until liquid is almost evaporated. Season with pepper. Stir in tomatoes, water, chickpeas and tomato paste; mix well.

2. Secure lid and move pressure release valve to Sealing position. Press Pressure Cook or Manual; cook at high pressure 22 minutes.

3. When cooking is complete, use natural release for 10 minutes, then release remaining pressure. Meanwhile, prepare Polenta, if desired.

4. Serve ragoût over Polenta.

Makes 6 servings

POLENTA: Combine 2 cups milk, 2 cups water and ¼ teaspoon salt in large saucepan; bring to a boil over medium-high heat. Slowly whisk in 1 cup instant polenta in thin steady stream. Cook 4 to 5 minutes or until thick and creamy, whisking constantly. Remove from heat; stir in ½ cup grated Parmesan cheese.

BLACK BEAN CHILI

1 **pound dried black beans, soaked 8 hours or overnight**

1 **tablespoon olive oil**

1 **large onion, chopped**

1 **large jalapeño pepper, minced**

3 **cloves garlic, minced**

2 **tablespoons chili powder**

2 **teaspoons salt**

1 **teaspoon paprika**

1 **teaspoon dried oregano**

1 **teaspoon unsweetened cocoa powder**

½ **teaspoon ground cumin**

¼ **teaspoon ground cinnamon**

2 **cups water**

1 **can (about 14 ounces) diced tomatoes**

1 **bay leaf**

1 **to 2 tablespoons lime juice**

Optional toppings: sour cream, picante sauce, sliced green onions, chopped fresh cilantro

1. Drain and rinse beans. Press Sauté; heat oil in Instant Pot. Add onion; cook and stir 5 minutes. Add jalapeño, garlic, chili powder, salt, paprika, oregano, cocoa, cumin and cinnamon; cook and stir 1 minute. Add beans, water, tomatoes and bay leaf; mix well.

2. Secure lid and move pressure release valve to Sealing position. Press Pressure Cook or Manual; cook at high pressure 8 minutes.

3. When cooking is complete, use natural release for 15 minutes, then release remaining pressure.

4. For thicker chili, press Sauté; cook 3 to 5 minutes or until chili thickens, stirring frequently. (Chili will also thicken upon standing.) Remove and discard bay leaf. Stir in lime juice; serve with desired toppings.

Makes 6 servings

TIP: For a heartier meal, hollow out small loaves of sourdough bread and serve the chili in bread bowls.

APPLE–CINNAMON BREAKFAST RISOTTO

4 tablespoons (½ stick) butter, divided

4 medium Granny Smith apples (about 1½ pounds), peeled and diced

1½ teaspoons ground cinnamon

1½ cups uncooked arborio rice, divided

1 teaspoon salt

¼ teaspoon ground allspice

4 cups apple juice

2 tablespoons packed dark brown sugar, plus additional for serving

1 teaspoon vanilla

Milk, sliced almonds and dried cranberries (optional)

1. Press Sauté; melt 2 tablespoos butter in Instant Pot. Add apples and ½ teaspoon cinnamon; cook and stir about 5 minutes or until apples are softened. Transfer to small bowl; set aside.

2. Melt remaining 2 tablespoons butter in pot. Add rice, remaining 1 teaspoon cinnamon, salt and allspice; cook and stir 1 minute. Stir in apple juice, 2 tablespoons brown sugar and vanilla; mix well.

3. Secure lid and move pressure release valve to Sealing position. Press Pressure Cook or Manual; cook at high pressure 6 minutes.

4. When cooking is complete, press Cancel and use quick release. Press Sauté; add reserved apples to pot. Cook and stir 1 minute or until risotto reaches desired consistency. Serve with milk, almonds, cranberries and additional brown sugar, if desired.

Makes 6 servings

CHEESY POLENTA

5 **cups vegetable or chicken broth**

½ **teaspoon salt**

1½ **cups uncooked instant polenta**

½ **cup grated Parmesan cheese**

¼ **cup (½ stick) butter, cubed, plus additional for serving**

Fried sage leaves (optional)

1. Combine broth and salt in Instant Pot; slowly whisk in polenta until blended.

2. Secure lid and move pressure release valve to Sealing position. Press Pressure Cook or Manual; cook at high pressure 5 minutes.

3. When cooking is complete, use natural release for 5 minutes, then release remaining pressure.

4. Whisk in cheese and ¼ cup butter until well blended. (Polenta may appear separated immediately after cooking but will come together when stirred.) Serve with additional butter; garnish with sage.

Makes 6 servings

TIP: Spread any leftover polenta in a baking dish and refrigerate until cold. Cut the cold polenta into sticks or slices, brush with olive oil and pan-fry or grill until lightly browned.

QUINOA AND MANGO SALAD

1 **cup uncooked quinoa**	½ **cup dried cranberries**
1½ **cups water**	2 **tablespoons chopped fresh parsley**
¾ **teaspoon salt, divided**	¼ **cup extra virgin olive oil**
2 **cups cubed peeled mango (about 2 large mangoes)**	1½ **tablespoons white wine vinegar**
½ **cup sliced green onions**	1 **teaspoon Dijon mustard**
	⅛ **teaspoon black pepper**

1. Place quinoa in fine-mesh strainer; rinse under cold running water and drain. Combine quinoa, 1½ cups water and ¼ teaspoon salt in Instant Pot; mix well.

2. Secure lid and move pressure release valve to Sealing position. Press Pressure Cook or Manual; cook at high pressure 1 minute.

3. When cooking is complete, use natural release for 10 minutes, then release remaining pressure.

4. Press Sauté; cook and stir 1 minute or until any excess water has evaporated. Spread quinoa on large plate or in baking dish; cover loosely and refrigerate at least 1 hour.

5. Add mangoes, green onions, cranberries and parsley to quinoa; mix well. Combine oil, vinegar, mustard, remaining ½ teaspoon salt and pepper in small bowl; whisk until blended. Pour over quinoa mixture; stir until well blended.

Makes 6 servings

TIP: This salad can be made several hours ahead and refrigerated. Let stand at room temperature for at least 30 minutes before serving.

SPINACH RISOTTO

2 tablespoons olive oil

2 tablespoons butter, divided

1 shallot, finely chopped

1½ cups uncooked arborio rice

1½ teaspoons salt

¼ teaspoon black pepper

½ cup dry white wine

4 cups vegetable broth

2 cups packed baby spinach

½ cup shredded Parmesan cheese

2 tablespoons pine nuts, toasted*

To toast pine nuts, cook in small skillet over medium heat 3 minutes or until lightly browned, stirring frequently.

1. Press Sauté; heat oil and 1 tablespoon butter in Instant Pot. Add shallot; cook and stir 2 minutes or until softened. Add rice; cook and stir 3 minutes or until rice is translucent. Stir in salt and pepper. Add wine; cook and stir about 1 minute or until evaporated. Stir in broth; mix well.

2. Secure lid and move pressure release valve to Sealing position. Press Pressure Cook or Manual; cook at high pressure 6 minutes.

3. When cooking is complete, press Cancel and use quick release.

4. Press Sauté; adjust heat to low ("less"). Add spinach to pot; cook about 3 minutes or until spinach is wilted and risotto reaches desired consistency, stirring constantly. Stir in cheese and remaining 1 tablespoon butter until blended. Sprinkle with pine nuts.

Makes 4 servings

CHICKPEA TIKKA MASALA

1¼ cups dried chickpeas, soaked 8 hours or overnight

1 tablespoon olive oil

1 onion, chopped

3 cloves garlic, minced

1 tablespoon minced fresh ginger or ginger paste

1 tablespoon garam masala

1½ teaspoons salt

1 teaspoon ground coriander

1 teaspoon ground cumin

¼ teaspoon ground red pepper

1 can (28 ounces) crushed tomatoes

1 can (about 13 ounces) coconut milk

1 package (about 12 ounces) paneer cheese, cut into 1-inch cubes

Hot cooked basmati rice (optional)

Chopped fresh cilantro (optional)

1. Drain and rinse chickpeas. Press Sauté; heat oil in Instant Pot. Add onion; cook and stir 5 minutes or until translucent. Add garlic, ginger, garam masala, salt, coriander, cumin and red pepper; cook and stir 1 minute. Stir in chickpeas, tomatoes and coconut milk; mix well.

2. Secure lid and move pressure release valve to Sealing position. Press Pressure Cook or Manual; cook at high pressure 22 minutes.

3. When cooking is complete, use natural release for 10 minutes, then release remaining pressure.

4. Press Sauté; adjust heat to low ("less"). Add paneer; stir gently. Cook 5 minutes or until paneer is heated through, stirring occasionally. Serve over rice, if desired; garnish with cilantro.

Makes 4 servings

VARIATION: For a vegan dish, substitute one package (about 12 ounces) firm silken tofu, drained and cut into 1-inch cubes, for the paneer.

PESTO RICE AND BEANS

½ cup dried Great Northern beans, soaked 8 hours or overnight

1½ cups water or chicken broth, divided

¼ teaspoon salt, divided

½ cup uncooked long grain rice

4 ounces fresh green beans, cut into 1-inch pieces (about ¾ cup)

¼ cup prepared pesto

Optional toppings: shredded Parmesan cheese, chopped plum tomatoes and chopped fresh parsley (optional)

1. Drain and rinse Great Northern beans. Combine Great Northern beans, 1 cup water and ⅛ teaspoon salt in Instant Pot; mix well. Secure lid and move pressure release valve to Sealing position. Press Pressure Cook or Manual; cook at high pressure 4 minutes.

2. Meanwhile, rinse rice well; drain in fine-mesh strainer. Combine rice, remaining ½ cup water and ⅛ teaspoon salt in small metal or ceramic bowl that fits inside pot; mix well. Place green beans in center of 12-inch square of foil; sprinkle with additional salt. Bring up two sides of foil over beans; fold foil over several times to create packet. Fold in opposite ends. (Packet should measure about 8×4 inches.)

3. When cooking of Great Northern beans is complete, press Cancel and use quick release. Place bowl with rice on rack; lower rack into pot. Arrange foil packet on top of bowl. (Packet should not entirely cover bowl.) Secure lid and move pressure release valve to Sealing position. Press Pressure Cook or Manual; cook at high pressure 4 minutes.

4. When cooking is complete, use natural release for 8 minutes, then release remaining pressure. Use handles of rack to remove bowl and foil packet from pot. If any liquid remains in bottom of pot with Great Northern beans, press Sauté; cook 1 to 2 minutes or until liquid is evaporated.

5. Add Great Northern beans and green beans to bowl with rice; gently stir in pesto. Top with cheese, tomatoes and parsley, if desired.

Makes 4 servings

SOUTHWESTERN MAC AND CHEESE

4   tablespoons (½ stick) butter, divided

1   onion, finely chopped

3⅓ cups water

1   package (16 ounces) uncooked elbow macaroni

1   can (about 14 ounces) diced tomatoes with green peppers and onions

1   teaspoon salt

4   cups (16 ounces) shredded Mexican cheese blend, divided

½   cup milk

1   cup salsa

1. Press Sauté; melt 1 tablespoon butter in Instant Pot. Add onion; cook and stir 3 minutes or until softened. Stir in water, macaroni, tomatoes and salt; mix well.

2. Secure lid and move pressure release valve to Sealing position. Press Pressure Cook or Manual; cook at high pressure 4 minutes.

3. When cooking is complete, press Cancel and use quick release.

4. Press Sauté; add 3½ cups cheese, milk and remaining 3 tablespoons butter to pot. Stir until smooth and well blended. Stir in salsa. Press Cancel. Sprinkle remaining ½ cup cheese over pasta; let stand until melted.

Makes 6 to 8 servings

CREAMY BARLEY RISOTTO

1 tablespoon olive oil

1 large leek, halved and thinly sliced

1 cup uncooked pearled barley

1 teaspoon salt

2 cups vegetable broth

¼ teaspoon black pepper

1 cup frozen peas

½ cup shredded Parmesan cheese

2 tablespoons butter, cut into pieces

1 tablespoon lemon juice

1 teaspoon grated lemon peel, plus additional for garnish

Shaved Parmesan cheese (optional)

Chopped fresh Italian parsley (optional)

1. Press Sauté; heat oil in Instant Pot. Add leek; cook and stir 3 minutes or until softened and beginning to brown. Add barley and salt; cook and stir 1 minute. Stir in broth and pepper; mix well.

2. Secure lid and move pressure release valve to Sealing position. Press Pressure Cook or Manual; cook at high pressure 18 minutes.

3. When cooking is complete, use natural release for 10 minutes, then release remaining pressure.

4. Press Sauté; stir in peas, ½ cup grated cheese, butter, lemon juice and 1 teaspoon lemon peel. Cook 1 minute or just until heated through. Garnish with shaved cheese, additional lemon peel and parsley.

Makes 4 servings

FRIJOLES BORRACHOS (DRUNKEN BEANS)

1 **pound dried pinto beans, soaked 8 hours or overnight**

6 **slices bacon, chopped**

1 **large onion, chopped**

3 **jalapeño peppers, seeded and finely chopped**

1 **tablespoon minced garlic**

1 **tablespoon dried oregano**

1 **cup dark Mexican beer**

1 **can (about 14 ounces) diced tomatoes**

1 **cup water**

¾ **teaspoon salt**

¼ **cup chopped fresh cilantro, plus additional for garnish**

1. Drain and rinse beans. Press Sauté; cook bacon in Instant Pot until crisp. Drain off all but 2 tablespoons drippings. Add onion to pot; cook and stir 4 minutes or until softened and lightly browned. Add jalapeños, garlic and oregano; cook and stir 1 minute. Stir in beer, scraping up browned bits from bottom of pot. Stir in beans, tomatoes, water and salt; mix well.

2. Secure lid and move pressure release valve to Sealing position. Press Pressure Cook or Manual; cook at high pressure 22 minutes.

3. When cooking is complete, use natural release for 10 minutes, then release remaining pressure.

4. Press Sauté; cook 3 minutes, mashing beans slightly until broth is thickened and creamy. Stir in ¼ cup cilantro. Garnish with additional cilantro.

Makes 6 to 8 servings

BULGUR PILAF WITH CARAMELIZED ONIONS AND KALE

1 tablespoon olive oil	2¾ cups vegetable or chicken broth
1 onion, cut into thin wedges	1 cup medium grain bulgur
1 clove garlic, minced	1 teaspoon salt
2 cups chopped kale	¼ teaspoon black pepper

1. Press Sauté; heat oil in Instant Pot. Add onion; cook about 10 minutes or until golden brown, stirring frequently. Add garlic; cook and stir 1 minute. Add kale; cook and stir about 1 minute or until wilted. Stir in broth, bulgur, salt and pepper; mix well.

2. Secure lid and move pressure release valve to Sealing position. Press Pressure Cook or Manual; cook at high pressure 8 minutes.

3. When cooking is complete, use natural release for 5 minutes, then release remaining pressure.

Makes 4 servings

WHITE CHICKEN CHILI

1 tablespoon vegetable oil

1½ pounds boneless skinless chicken breasts

2 medium onions, chopped

1 can (4 ounces) diced mild green chiles

1 tablespoon minced garlic

2 teaspoons ground cumin

1 teaspoon salt

1 teaspoon dried oregano

¼ teaspoon black pepper

¼ teaspoon ground red pepper

1½ cups chicken broth

2 cans (about 15 ounces each) Great Northern beans, rinsed and drained

¼ cup chopped fresh cilantro

1. Press Sauté; heat oil in Instant Pot. Add chicken; cook about 6 minutes or until browned on both sides. Remove to plate. Add onion and chiles to pot; cook and stir 3 minutes. Add garlic, cumin, salt, oregano, black pepper and red pepper; cook and stir 1 minute. Stir in broth, scraping up browned bits from bottom of pot. Stir in beans. Return chicken to pot, pressing into liquid.

2. Secure lid and move pressure release valve to Sealing position. Press Pressure Cook or Manual; cook at high pressure 7 minutes.

3. When cooking is complete, press Cancel and use quick release. Remove chicken to clean plate; set aside until cool enough to handle.

4. Shred chicken into bite-size pieces; return to pot. Press Sauté; cook 2 to 3 minutes or until chili thickens slightly. Sprinkle with cilantro.

Makes 6 servings

PUMPKIN RISOTTO

2 tablespoons butter

1 tablespoon olive oil

1 onion, finely chopped

2 cloves garlic, minced

1½ cups uncooked arborio rice

1 teaspoon salt

¼ teaspoon ground nutmeg

⅛ teaspoon black pepper

½ cup dry white wine

4 cups vegetable broth

1 can (15 ounces) solid-pack pumpkin

5 fresh sage leaves

½ cup shredded Parmesan cheese, plus additional for serving

¼ cup roasted pumpkin seeds (pepitas)

1. Press Sauté; heat butter and oil in Instant Pot. Add onion and garlic; cook and stir 3 minutes or until softened. Add rice; cook and stir 4 minutes or until rice is translucent. Stir in salt, nutmeg and pepper. Add wine; cook and stir about 1 minute or until evaporated. Stir in broth, pumpkin and sage; mix well.

2. Secure lid and move pressure release valve to Sealing position. Press Pressure Cook or Manual; cook at high pressure 6 minutes.

3. When cooking is complete, press Cancel and use quick release.

4. Press Sauté; adjust heat to low ("less"). Cook about 3 minutes or until risotto reaches desired consistency, stirring constantly. Stir in ½ cup cheese until blended. Serve immediately with additional cheese and pumpkin seeds.

Makes 4 servings

SUPERFOOD BREAKFAST PORRIDGE

¾ **cup steel-cut oats**

¼ **cup uncooked quinoa, rinsed and drained**

¼ **cup dried cranberries, plus additional for serving**

¼ **cup raisins**

3 **tablespoons ground flax seeds**

2 **tablespoons chia seeds**

1 **teaspoon olive oil**

¼ **teaspoon salt**

¼ **teaspoon ground cinnamon**

2½ **cups almond milk, plus additional for serving**

1½ **cups water**

Maple syrup (optional)

¼ **cup sliced almonds, toasted* (optional)**

*To toast almonds, cook and stir in small skillet over medium heat 1 to 2 minutes or until lightly browned.

1. Spray heatproof bowl (metal, glass or ceramic) that fits inside of Instant Pot with nonstick cooking spray. Combine oats, quinoa, ¼ cup cranberries, raisins, flax seeds, chia seeds, oil, salt and cinnamon in prepared bowl; mix well. Stir in 2½ cups almond milk until blended.

2. Pour water into pot. Place rack in pot; place bowl on rack. Secure lid and move pressure release valve to Sealing position. Press Pressure Cook or Manual; cook at high pressure 13 minutes.

3. When cooking is complete, use natural release.

4. Stir porridge until smooth. Serve with additional almond milk, cranberries, maple syrup and almonds, if desired.

Makes 4 servings

BARLEY WITH CURRANTS AND PINE NUTS

2 **tablespoons butter**

1 **onion, finely chopped**

2 **cups vegetable broth**

1 **cup uncooked pearled barley**

½ **cup currants**

½ **teaspoon salt**

¼ **teaspoon black pepper**

2 **ounces (about ½ cup) pine nuts, toasted***

*To toast pine nuts, cook in small skillet over medium heat 3 minutes or until lightly browned, stirring frequently.

1. Press Sauté; melt butter in Instant Pot. Add onion; cook and stir 5 minutes or until tender. Stir in broth, barley, currants, salt and pepper; mix well.

2. Secure lid and move pressure release valve to Sealing position. Press Pressure Cook or Manual; cook at high pressure 18 minutes.

3. When cooking is complete, use natural release for 10 minutes, then release remaining pressure.

4. Stir in pine nuts. Serve warm or at room temperature.

Makes 4 to 6 servings

CHEESE GRITS WITH CHILES AND BACON

6 slices bacon, chopped

1 large shallot or small onion, finely chopped

1 serrano or jalapeño pepper, minced

3½ cups chicken broth

1 cup uncooked grits*

½ teaspoon salt

¼ teaspoon black pepper

1 cup (4 ounces) shredded Cheddar cheese

½ cup half-and-half

2 tablespoons finely chopped green onion

Do not use instant grits.

1. Press Sauté; cook bacon in Instant Pot until crisp. Drain on paper towel-lined plate. Drain off all but 1 tablespoon drippings.

2. Add shallot and serrano pepper to pot; cook and stir 2 minutes or until shallot is lightly browned. Add broth, grits, salt and black pepper; cook and stir 1 minute.

3. Secure lid and move pressure release valve to Sealing position. Press Pressure Cook or Manual; cook at high pressure 14 minutes.

4. When cooking is complete, use natural release for 10 minutes, then release remaining pressure.

5. Stir grits until smooth. Add cheese, half-and-half and half of bacon; stir until well blended. Sprinkle with green onion and remaining bacon.

Makes 4 servings

WARM CHOCOLATE CAKES

½ cup (1 stick) butter, cut into pieces

4 ounces bittersweet chocolate, chopped

½ teaspoon espresso powder or instant coffee granules

1 cup powdered sugar, plus additional for garnish

2 eggs

2 egg yolks

1 teaspoon vanilla

⅓ cup all-purpose flour

¼ teaspoon salt

1 cup water

1. Combine butter, chocolate and espresso powder in small saucepan; heat over very low heat until mixture is melted and smooth, stirring frequently. Whisk in 1 cup powdered sugar until well blended. Add eggs, egg yolks and vanilla; whisk until blended. Add flour and salt; whisk until blended. Divide batter among four 6-ounce ramekins or custard cups.

2. Pour water into Instant Pot; place rack in pot. Arrange ramekins on rack, stacking as necessary.

3. Secure lid and move pressure release valve to Sealing position. Press Pressure Cook or Manual; cook at high pressure 9 minutes.

4. When cooking is complete, press Cancel and use quick release.

5. Remove ramekins from pot. Gently dab paper towel over tops of cakes to remove any condensation. Sprinkle with additional powdered sugar; serve warm.

Makes 4 servings

PUMPKIN BREAD PUDDING

1 cup whole milk
2 eggs
½ cup canned pumpkin
⅓ cup packed brown sugar
1 tablespoon butter, melted
1½ teaspoons ground cinnamon
1 teaspoon vanilla
¼ teaspoon salt
¼ teaspoon ground nutmeg
8 slices cinnamon raisin bread, torn into small pieces (about 4 cups)
1¼ cups water
 Bourbon Caramel Sauce (recipe follows, optional)

1. Spray 6- to 7-inch (1½-quart) soufflé dish or round baking dish that fits inside Instant Pot with nonstick cooking spray. Whisk milk, eggs, pumpkin, brown sugar, butter, cinnamon, vanilla, salt and nutmeg in large bowl until well blended. Add bread cubes; toss to coat. Pour into prepared dish; cover tightly with foil.

2. Pour water into pot. Place soufflé dish on rack; lower rack into pot.

3. Secure lid and move pressure release valve to Sealing position. Press Pressure Cook or Manual; cook at high pressure 40 minutes.

4. When cooking is complete, use natural release for 10 minutes, then release remaining pressure.

5. Remove soufflé dish from pot. Remove foil; cool 15 minutes. Meanwhile, prepare Bourbon Caramel Sauce, if desired. Serve bread pudding warm with sauce.

Makes 4 servings

BOURBON CARAMEL SAUCE: Combine ¼ cup (½ stick) butter, ¼ cup packed brown sugar and ¼ cup whipping cream in small saucepan; bring to a boil over high heat, stirring frequently. Remove from heat; stir in 1 tablespoon bourbon.

APPLESAUCE CUSTARD

1½ cups unsweetened applesauce

½ teaspoon ground cinnamon

¼ teaspoon salt

4 eggs, at room temperature

½ cup half-and-half

¼ cup unsweetened apple juice concentrate

⅛ teaspoon ground nutmeg

1¼ cups water

1. Combine applesauce, cinnamon and salt in medium bowl; mix well. Whisk in eggs, half-and-half and apple juice concentrate until well blended. Pour into 1½-quart soufflé dish or round baking dish that fits inside Instant Pot. Sprinkle with nutmeg. Cover dish tightly with foil.

2. Pour water into pot. Place soufflé dish on rack; lower rack into pot.

3. Secure lid and move pressure release valve to Sealing position. Press Pressure Cook or Manual; cook at high pressure 30 minutes.

4. When cooking is complete, use natural release for 10 minutes, then release remaining pressure.

5. Remove soufflé dish from pot. Remove foil; cool to room temperature. Serve custard at room temperature or chilled.

Makes 6 servings

PEANUT BUTTER PUDDING

2 cups milk

2 eggs

⅓ cup creamy peanut butter

¼ cup packed brown sugar

¼ teaspoon vanilla

1 cup water

Shaved chocolate or shredded coconut (optional)

1. Spray six 3-ounce ramekins or custard cups with nonstick cooking spray. Combine milk, eggs, peanut butter, brown sugar and vanilla in blender; blend at high speed 1 minute. Pour into prepared custard cups. Cover each ramekin tightly with foil.

2. Pour water into Instant Pot; place rack in pot. Arrange ramekins on rack, stacking as necessary.

3. Secure lid and move pressure release valve to Sealing position. Press Pressure Cook or Manual; cook at high pressure 8 minutes.

4. When cooking is complete, use natural release for 10 minutes, then release remaining pressure.

5. Remove ramekins from pot. Remove foil; cool to room temperature. Refrigerate until chilled. Garnish with shaved chocolate.

Makes 6 servings

CHOCOLATE SURPRISE CRÈME BRÛLÉE

3 ounces bittersweet chocolate, finely chopped

5 egg yolks

1¾ cups whipping cream

½ cup granulated sugar

¼ teaspoon salt

1 teaspoon vanilla

1 cup water

¼ cup demerara or raw sugar

1. Spray bottoms of five 6-ounce ramekins or custard cups with nonstick cooking spray. Divide chocolate evenly among ramekins.

2. Whisk egg yolks in medium bowl. Combine cream, granulated sugar and salt in medium saucepan; bring to a simmer over medium heat. Slowly pour ¼ cup hot cream mixture into egg yolks, whisking until blended. Add remaining cream mixture in thin, steady stream, whisking constantly. Pour through fine-mesh strainer into clean bowl. Stir in vanilla. Ladle custard mixture into prepared ramekins over chocolate. Cover each ramekin tightly with foil.

3. Pour water into Instant Pot; place rack in pot. Arrange ramekins on rack, stacking as necessary.

4. Secure lid and move pressure release valve to Sealing position. Press Pressure Cook or Manual; cook at high pressure 6 minutes.

5. When cooking is complete, use natural release for 10 minutes, then release remaining pressure. Remove ramekins from pot. Remove foil; cool to room temperature. Refrigerate until ready to serve.

6. Just before serving, preheat broiler. Place ramekins on baking sheet; sprinkle tops of custards with demerara sugar. Broil 4 inches from heat 1 to 2 minutes or until sugar bubbles and browns.

Makes 5 servings

ESPRESSO CRÈME BRÛLÉE: Reduce cream to 1½ cups and add ¼ cup espresso. Heat mixture in saucepan with sugar and salt as directed in step 2.

QUICK AND EASY KHEER
(INDIAN RICE PUDDING)

3 cups whole milk

⅔ cup sugar

1 cup uncooked basmati rice, rinsed and drained

½ cup golden raisins

3 whole green cardamom pods *or* ¼ teaspoon ground cardamon

¼ teaspoon salt

Grated orange peel (optional)

Pistachio nuts (optional)

1. Combine milk and sugar in Instant Pot; stir until sugar is dissolved. Add rice, raisins, cardamom and salt; mix well.

2. Secure lid and move pressure release valve to Sealing position. Press Pressure Cook or Manual; cook at high pressure 5 minutes.

3. When cooking is complete, use natural release for 10 minutes, then release remaining pressure.

4. Stir rice pudding well before serving. (Pudding will thicken upon standing.) Garnish with orange peel and pistachios.

Makes 6 to 8 servings

VERY BERRY CHEESECAKE

CRUST
¾ **cup honey graham cracker crumbs (about 5 whole crackers)**

3 **tablespoons butter, melted**

CHEESECAKE
2 **packages (8 ounces each) cream cheese, at room temperature**

½ **cup sugar**

2 **eggs, at room temperature**

1 **teaspoon vanilla**

1 **cup fresh blueberries**

2 **cups water**

TOPPING
½ **cup seedless raspberry jam**

1 **cup fresh raspberries**

1. Cut parchment paper to fit bottom of 7-inch springform pan. Lightly spray bottom and side of pan with nonstick cooking spray. Wrap outside of pan with foil.

2. Combine graham cracker crumbs and melted butter in small bowl; mix well. Pat mixture onto bottom and about ½ inch up side of prepared pan. Freeze 10 minutes.

3. Beat cream cheese and sugar in large bowl with electric mixer at medium-high speed until light and fluffy. Add eggs, one at a time, beating well after each addition. Stir in vanilla. Sprinkle blueberries over crust; pour batter over blueberries. Cover pan tightly with foil.

4. Pour water into Instant Pot. Place pan on rack; lower rack into pot. Secure lid and move pressure release valve to Sealing position. Press Pressure Cook or Manual; cook at high pressure 33 minutes.

5. When cooking is complete, press Cancel and use quick release. Use handles on rack to lift pan from pot. Remove foil; cool 1 hour. Run thin knife around edge of cheesecake to loosen (do not remove side of pan). Refrigerate 2 to 3 hours or overnight.

6. Remove side and bottom of pan; transfer cheesecake to serving plate, if desired. Heat jam in small saucepan over low heat or in glass measuring cup in microwave, stirring until smooth. Spoon melted jam over cheesecake; top with raspberries.

Makes 6 to 8 servings

PLUM BREAD PUDDING

6 **cups cubed brioche, egg bread or challah (1-inch cubes)**

1½ **tablespoons butter**

2 **large plums, pitted and cut into thin wedges**

⅓ **cup plus ½ tablespoon sugar, divided**

3 **eggs**

¾ **cup half-and-half**

½ **cup milk**

½ **teaspoon vanilla**

¼ **teaspoon salt**

¼ **teaspoon ground cinnamon**

1¼ **cups water**

Whipping cream or vanilla ice cream (optional)

1. Preheat oven to 400°F. Spray 6- to 7-inch (1½-quart) soufflé dish or round baking dish that fits inside Instant Pot with nonstick cooking spray.

2. Spread bread cubes in single layer on ungreased baking sheet. Bake 6 to 7 minutes or until lightly toasted, stirring halfway through baking time.

3. Meanwhile, melt butter in large skillet over medium-high heat. Add plums and ½ tablespoon sugar; cook 2 minutes or until plums are softened and release juices. Beat eggs in large bowl. Add half-and-half, milk, remaining ⅓ cup sugar, vanilla, salt and cinnamon; mix well. Add plums and toasted bread cubes; stir gently to coat. Pour into prepared soufflé dish. Cover dish tightly with foil.

4. Pour water into pot. Place soufflé dish on rack; lower rack into pot.

5. Secure lid and move pressure release valve to Sealing position. Press Pressure Cook or Manual; cook at high pressure 35 minutes. When cooking is complete, use natural release for 10 minutes, then release remaining pressure.

6. Remove soufflé dish from pot. Let stand, covered, 15 minutes. Remove foil; serve warm with cream, if desired.

Makes 6 servings

CUSTARD BRÛLÉE

5 egg yolks
½ cup granulated sugar
¼ teaspoon salt
1 cup whipping cream
1 cup milk

1 teaspoon vanilla
¼ teaspoon ground cinnamon
  Ground nutmeg (optional)
1¼ cups water
¼ cup packed brown sugar

1. Whisk egg yolks, granulated sugar and salt in medium bowl until blended. Add cream, milk and vanilla; whisk until well blended. Pour into 6- to 7-inch (1½-quart) soufflé dish or round casserole that fits inside Instant Pot. Sprinkle with cinnamon and nutmeg, if desired. Cover dish tightly with foil.

2. Pour water into pot. Place soufflé dish on rack; lower rack into pot.

3. Secure lid and move pressure release valve to Sealing position. Press Pressure Cook or Manual; cook at high pressure 35 minutes.

4. When cooking is complete, press Cancel and use quick release.

5. Remove soufflé dish from pot. Remove foil; cool to room temperature. Cover and refrigerate 3 to 4 hours or until chilled.

6. Just before serving, preheat broiler. Sprinkle brown sugar evenly over top of custard. Broil 4 inches from heat 1 to 2 minutes or until sugar bubbles and browns.

Makes 6 to 8 servings

FUDGY CHOCOLATE PUDDING CAKE

- ¾ cup plus ⅓ cup granulated sugar, divided
- 1 cup all-purpose flour
- ¼ cup plus 3 tablespoons unsweetened cocoa powder, divided
- 2 teaspoons baking powder
- ¼ teaspoon salt
- ½ cup milk
- ⅓ cup butter, melted
- 1 teaspoon vanilla
- ½ cup packed brown sugar
- 1 cup hot water
- 1¼ cups water
- Vanilla ice cream (optional)

1. Spray 6- to 7-inch (1½-quart) soufflé dish or round baking dish that fits inside Instant Pot with nonstick cooking spray.

2. Combine ¾ cup granulated sugar, flour, ¼ cup cocoa, baking powder and salt in medium bowl; mix well. Add milk, butter and vanilla; whisk until well blended. Spread batter in prepared soufflé dish; smooth top. Combine brown sugar, remaining ⅓ cup granulated sugar and 3 tablespoons cocoa in small bowl; mix well. Sprinkle evenly over batter. Pour 1 cup hot water over top. (Do not stir.)

3. Pour 1¼ cups water into pot. Place soufflé dish on rack; lower rack into pot.

4. Secure lid and move pressure release valve to Sealing position. Press Pressure Cook or Manual; cook at high pressure 40 minutes.

5. When cooking is complete, use natural release for 10 minutes, then release remaining pressure.

6. Remove soufflé dish from pot; let stand 5 minutes. Serve warm with ice cream, if desired.

Makes 6 servings

CINNAMON RAISIN BREAD PUDDING

4 **to 5 cups cubed day-old French bread (1-inch cubes)**

1 **cup raisins**

2 **cups milk**

2 **eggs**

1 **egg yolk**

¼ **cup sugar**

⅛ **teaspoon ground cinnamon**

⅛ **teaspoon ground nutmeg**

1¼ **cups water**

Vanilla Rum Sauce (recipe follows, optional)

1. Spray 1½-quart soufflé dish or round baking dish that fits inside Instant Pot with nonstick cooking spray. Combine bread cubes and raisins in prepared dish; toss to distribute raisins evenly.

2. Whisk milk, eggs, egg yolk, sugar, cinnamon and nutmeg in medium bowl until well blended. Pour over bread mixture; press bread down into liquid. Cover dish tightly with foil; let stand 15 minutes.

3. Pour water into pot. Place soufflé dish on rack; lower rack into pot.

4. Secure lid and move pressure release valve to Sealing position. Press Pressure Cook or Manual; cook at high pressure 35 minutes. Meanwhile, prepare Vanilla Rum Sauce, if desired.

5. When cooking is complete, use natural release for 10 minutes, then release remaining pressure.

6. Remove soufflé dish from pot. Remove foil; serve bread pudding warm with sauce.

Makes 6 to 8 servings

VANILLA RUM SAUCE: Beat 2 egg yolks and ¼ cup sugar in small bowl until light and fluffy. Heat 1 cup whipping cream to a simmer in medium saucepan over medium-high heat. Slowly add egg yolk mixture, whisking constantly 2 minutes. Remove from heat; strain into medium bowl. Stir in 2 tablespoons dark rum or brandy and ¼ teaspoon vanilla. Serve warm or at room temperature.

PUMPKIN CUSTARD

3 eggs

1 can (15 ounces) solid-pack pumpkin

1 can (14 ounces) sweetened condensed milk (NOT evaporated milk)

1 teaspoon ground cinnamon, plus additional for garnish

1 teaspoon finely chopped candied ginger *or* ½ teaspoon ground ginger

¼ teaspoon ground cloves

⅛ teaspoon salt

1 cup water

Whipped cream (optional)

1. Whisk eggs in medium bowl. Add pumpkin, sweetened condensed milk, 1 teaspoon cinnamon, ginger, cloves and salt; whisk until well blended and smooth. Pour into six 6-ounce ramekins or custard cups. Cover each ramekin tightly with foil.

2. Pour water into Instant Pot; place rack in pot. Arrange ramekins on rack, stacking as necessary.

3. Secure lid and move pressure release valve to Sealing position. Press Pressure Cook or Manual; cook at high pressure 8 minutes.

4. When cooking is complete, use natural release.

5. Remove ramekins from pot. Remove foil; cool to room temperature. Refrigerate until chilled. Top with whipped cream and additional cinnamon, if desired.

Makes 6 servings

RICH CHOCOLATE PUDDING

1½ **cups whipping cream**

4 **ounces bittersweet chocolate, chopped**

4 **egg yolks**

⅓ **cup packed brown sugar**

1 **tablespoon unsweetened cocoa powder**

1 **teaspoon vanilla**

¼ **teaspoon salt**

1¼ **cups water**

1. Heat cream to a simmer in medium saucepan over medium heat. Remove from heat. Add chocolate; stir until chocolate is melted and mixture is smooth.

2. Whisk egg yolks, brown sugar, cocoa, vanilla and salt in large bowl until well blended. Gradually add warm chocolate mixture, whisking constantly until blended. Strain into 6- to 7-inch (1½-quart) soufflé dish or round baking dish that fits inside Instant Pot. Cover dish tightly with foil.

3. Pour water into pot. Place soufflé dish on rack; lower rack into pot.

4. Secure lid and move pressure release valve to Sealing position. Press Pressure Cook or Manual; cook at low pressure 22 minutes.

5. When cooking is complete, use natural release for 5 minutes, then release remaining pressure.

6. Remove soufflé dish from pot. Remove foil; cool to room temperature. Cover and refrigerate at least 3 hours or up to 2 days.

Makes 6 servings

SUPERFAST APPLESAUCE

2   **pounds (about 4 medium) sweet apples (such as Fuji, Gala or Honeycrisp), peeled and cut into 1-inch pieces**

2   **pounds (about 4 medium) Granny Smith apples, peeled and cut into 1-inch pieces**

⅓   **cup water**

2   **to 4 tablespoons packed brown sugar**

1   **tablespoon lemon juice**

1   **teaspoon ground cinnamon**

⅛   **teaspoon salt**

⅛   **teaspoon ground nutmeg**

⅛   **teaspoon ground cloves**

1. Combine apples, water, 2 tablespoons brown sugar, lemon juice, cinnamon, salt, nutmeg and cloves in Instant Pot; mix well.

2. Secure lid and move pressure release valve to Sealing position. Press Pressure Cook or Manual; cook at high pressure 4 minutes.

3. When cooking is complete, press Cancel and use quick release.

4. Stir applesauce; taste for seasoning and add remaining 2 tablespoons brown sugar, if desired. If there is excess liquid in pot, press Sauté and cook 2 to 3 minutes or until liquid evaporates. Cool completely before serving.

Makes 4 cups

PRESSURE COOKING TIMES

POULTRY	Minutes Under Pressure	Pressure	Release
Chicken Breasts, Bone-in	7 to 10	High	Quick
Chicken Breasts, Boneless	5 to 8	High	Quick
Chicken Thigh, Bone-in	10 to 14	High	Natural
Chicken Thigh, Boneless	8 to 10	High	Natural
Chicken Wings	10 to 12	High	Quick
Chicken, Whole	22 to 26	High	Natural
Eggs, Hard-Cooked (3 to 12)	9	Low	Quick
Turkey Breast, Bone-in	25 to 30	High	Natural
Turkey Breast, Boneless	15 to 20	High	Natural
Turkey Legs	35 to 40	High	Natural
Turkey, Ground	8 to 10	High	Quick

MEAT

MEAT	Minutes Under Pressure	Pressure	Release
Beef, Bone-in Short Ribs	35 to 45	High	Natural
Beef, Brisket	60 to 75	High	Natural
Beef, Ground	8	High	Natural
Beef, Roast (round, rump or shoulder)	60 to 70	High	Natural
Beef, Stew Meat	20 to 25	High	Natural or Quick
Lamb, Chops	5 to 10	High	Quick
Lamb, Leg or Shanks	35 to 40	High	Natural
Lamb, Stew Meat	12 to 15	High	Quick
Pork, Baby Back Ribs	25 to 30	High	Natural
Pork, Chops	7 to 10	High	Quick
Pork, Ground	5	High	Quick
Pork, Loin	15 to 25	High	Natural
Pork, Shoulder or Butt	45 to 60	High	Natural
Pork, Stew Meat	15 to 20	High	Quick

SEAFOOD

SEAFOOD	Minutes Under Pressure	Pressure	Release
Cod	2 to 3	Low	Quick
Crab	2 to 3	Low	Quick
Halibut	6	Low	Quick
Mussels	1 to 2	Low	Quick
Salmon	4 to 5	Low	Quick
Scallops	1	Low	Quick
Shrimp	2 to 3	Low	Quick
Swordfish	4 to 5	Low	Quick
Tilapia	3	Low	Quick

VEGETABLES

VEGETABLES	Minutes Under Pressure	Pressure	Release
Artichokes, Whole	9 to 12	High	Natural
Beets, Medium Whole	18 to 24	High	Quick
Brussels Sprouts, Whole	2 to 3	High	Quick
Cabbage, Sliced	3 to 5	High	Quick
Carrots, Sliced	2 to 4	High	Quick
Cauliflower, Florets	2 to 3	High	Quick
Cauliflower, Whole	3 to 5	High	Quick

VEGETABLES	Minutes Under Pressure	Pressure	Release
Corn on the Cob	2 to 4	High	Quick
Eggplant	3 to 4	High	Quick
Fennel, Sliced	3 to 4	High	Quick
Green Beans	2 to 4	High	Quick
Kale	3	High	Quick
Leeks	3	High	Quick
Okra	3	High	Quick
Potatoes, Baby or Fingerling	6 to 10	High	Natural
Potatoes, New	7 to 9	High	Natural
Potatoes, 1-inch pieces	4 to 6	High	Quick
Potatoes, Sweet, 1-inch pieces	3	High	Quick
Potatoes, Sweet, Whole	8 to 12	High	Natural
Spinach	1	High	Quick
Squash, Acorn, Halved	7	High	Natural
Squash, Butternut, 1-inch pieces	4 to 6	High	Quick
Squash, Spaghetti, Halved	6 to 10	High	Natural
Tomatoes, cut into pieces for sauce	5	High	Natural

GRAINS

GRAINS	Liquid per cup	Minutes under pressure	Pressure	Release
Barley, Pearled	2	18 to 22	High	Natural
Barley, Whole	2½	30 to 35	High	Natural
Bulgur	3	8	High	Natural
Farro	2	10 to 12	High	Natural
Grits, Medium	4	12 to 15	High	10 minute natural
Millet	1½	1	High	Natural
Oats, Rolled	2	4 to 5	High	10 minute natural
Oats, Steel-Cut	3	10 to 13	High	10 minute natural
Quinoa	1½	1	High	10 minute natural
Polenta, Instant	3	5	High	5 minute natural
Rice, Arborio	2	6 to 7	High	Quick
Rice, Brown	1	22	High	10 minute natural
Rice, White Long Grain	1	4	High	10 minute natural

DRIED BEANS AND LEGUMES

	Unsoaked	Soaked	Pressure	Release
Black Beans	22 to 25	8 to 10	High	Natural
Black-Eyed Peas	9 to 11	3 to 5	High	Natural
Cannellini Beans	30 to 35	8 to 10	High	Natural
Chickpeas	35 to 40	18 to 22	High	Natural
Great Northern Beans	25 to 30	7 to 10	High	Natural
Kidney Beans	20 to 25	8 to 12	High	Natural
Lentils, Brown or Green	10 to 12	n/a	High	Natural
Lentils, Red or Yellow Split	1	n/a	High	Natural
Navy Beans	20 to 25	7 to 8	High	Natural
Pinto Beans	22 to 25	8 to 10	High	Natural
Split Peas	8 to 10	n/a	High	Natural

METRIC CONVERSION CHART

VOLUME MEASUREMENTS (dry)

¹/₈ teaspoon = 0.5 mL
¹/₄ teaspoon = 1 mL
¹/₂ teaspoon = 2 mL
³/₄ teaspoon = 4 mL
1 teaspoon = 5 mL
1 tablespoon = 15 mL
2 tablespoons = 30 mL
¹/₄ cup = 60 mL
¹/₃ cup = 75 mL
¹/₂ cup = 125 mL
²/₃ cup = 150 mL
³/₄ cup = 175 mL
1 cup = 250 mL
2 cups = 1 pint = 500 mL
3 cups = 750 mL
4 cups = 1 quart = 1 L

VOLUME MEASUREMENTS (fluid)

1 fluid ounce (2 tablespoons) = 30 mL
4 fluid ounces (¹/₂ cup) = 125 mL
8 fluid ounces (1 cup) = 250 mL
12 fluid ounces (1¹/₂ cups) = 375 mL
16 fluid ounces (2 cups) = 500 mL

WEIGHTS (mass)

¹/₂ ounce = 15 g
1 ounce = 30 g
3 ounces = 90 g
4 ounces = 120 g
8 ounces = 225 g
10 ounces = 285 g
12 ounces = 360 g
16 ounces = 1 pound = 450 g

DIMENSIONS

¹/₁₆ inch = 2 mm
¹/₈ inch = 3 mm
¹/₄ inch = 6 mm
¹/₂ inch = 1.5 cm
³/₄ inch = 2 cm
1 inch = 2.5 cm

OVEN TEMPERATURES

250°F = 120°C
275°F = 140°C
300°F = 150°C
325°F = 160°C
350°F = 180°C
375°F = 190°C
400°F = 200°C
425°F = 220°C
450°F = 230°C

BAKING PAN SIZES

Utensil	Size in Inches/Quarts	Metric Volume	Size in Centimeters
Baking or	8×8×2	2 L	20×20×5
Cake Pan	9×9×2	2.5 L	23×23×5
(square or	12×8×2	3 L	30×20×5
rectangular)	13×9×2	3.5 L	33×23×5
Loaf Pan	8×4×3	1.5 L	20×10×7
	9×5×3	2 L	23×13×7
Round Layer	8×1½	1.2 L	20×4
Cake Pan	9×1½	1.5 L	23×4
Pie Plate	8×1¼	750 mL	20×3
	9×1¼	1 L	23×3
Baking Dish	1 quart	1 L	—
or Casserole	1½ quart	1.5 L	—
	2 quart	2 L	—